a pima past

Anna Moore Shaw recounts Pima legends
outside the youth home at Salt River.

a pima past

anna moore shaw

The University of Arizona Press
Tucson, Arizona

About the Author . . .

ANNA MOORE SHAW, author of the book *Pima Indian Legends* (UA Press 1968), was born in a traditional brush dwelling on the Gila River Reservation in 1898. Her parents' conversion to Christianity prompted them to send her to school, and in 1920 she received her high-school diploma and married Ross Shaw, a Pima-Maricopa. After more than forty years of distinguished civic and religious activity in Phoenix, the couple returned to the Salt River Reservation, where they focused their attention on Indian problems. Anna has been on the Mutual Self-Help Housing Commission, edited the Pima newsletter, and taught kindergarten classes in Pima language and culture. One of the founders of the reservation's museum, she has served her tribe in many decision-making capacities.

THE UNIVERSITY OF ARIZONA PRESS

I.S.B.N.-0-8165-0426-1
L.C. No. 73-87716

To my family —
My beloved husband Ross
Our children Roderick, Adeline, and William
Our eleven grandchildren,
and our great-grandchildren

Contents

ILLUSTRATIONS

Foreword

RICH AND ABUNDANT as this book is in description of Pima
life ways, its major value lies in the personality of Mrs.
Shaw, who probably represents the typical, if there is one,
Pima life experience of the twentieth century. She is very
much a culturally assimilated Presbyterian Pima. Frequently she gives wonderful insights into just what the
"Pima" part of such a label means — the humor, a special
kind of humbleness, an insistent pride. Although strongly
influenced by Anglo institutions, she remains uniquely
Indian and proudly Piman.

Mrs. Shaw's story is primarily an autobiography in the
style of a family saga. Beginning with her grandfather in
the time of the very influential "Chief" Antonio Azul,
she brings us through her father's generation into her own,
concluding with her ideas concerning material progress
on the Salt River Reservation in the 1970s.

Throughout the unfolding of the events of her family's
lives, Mrs. Shaw seeks to integrate Pima customs, beliefs,
and legends into her story. Highly aware of the cultural
cross-currents affecting herself and her people, she treats
with particular sensitivity the major changes in lifestyle

which resulted from the coming of the Presbyterian missionaries at the end of the nineteenth century.

The story of the conversion of her father and his family provides insights into the processes of acceptance of good middle-class Anglo Presbyterian values so pervasive among this group of Pimas, the results of which are apparent at a Christmas dinner celebration at Gila River. A devoted convert, Mrs. Shaw's father, Josiah Moore, became a leading elder of the Gila Crossing Presbyterian Church. His children and several of his grandchildren went on to become leaders and models with respect to assimilation of Anglo culture, without loss of essential Pima identity.

Because she comes from this outstanding family important in Pima history and development and has led a more than ordinarily interesting life herself, Mrs. Shaw's autobiography takes on unusual value. Added social dimensions result from her associations with the most distinguished of those Pimas who have followed a similar path and her vigorous commitment to preserving selected elements of the traditional Indian culture while bringing a higher standard of living, in Anglo terms, to her reservation. Taken as a whole, her little book makes an important contribution to our understanding of the Pima past.

EDWARD H. SPICER

Introducing Anna Moore Shaw

by Anne Phelps Kopta

ANNA MOORE WAS BORN in a brush house in the village of Santa Cruz on the Gila River Reservation near Phoenix, Arizona, in 1898. Although her parents had no formal schooling, they bequeathed to their daughter Anna and to her brother, William Moore, the priceless basic principles of living that are all too often not taught to the young people of today — white or Indian. They educated their son and daughter in all those matters which have made each of them capable of establishing homes of their own.

Anna was a student in my classes at the Phoenix Indian boarding school from 1908–18. Her experience with academic subjects was extremely satisfactory. The courses of study at the school were not designed to make whites of Indians, as is sometimes charged, but to give young Indian students a basic education in the three R's, to acquaint them with the rudiments of many different trades, and to introduce them to the world off the Indian reservation.

The real value of such an education contributes to the general personal growth of the student, and it is always gratifying that an appreciable number of these Indians can and do discover who they are as individuals and thus learn what they would like to contribute to the world.

After graduating from the Indian School, Anna attended Phoenix Union High School. She received her diploma and married Ross Shaw, a former classmate and childhood sweetheart who had just returned from overseas service in World War I.

The following years were happy and very busy ones as the couple maintained a home in Phoenix and reared a family of two boys and a girl. Anna passed on to her children the many legends of the Pimas and a knowledge of the ancient customs and traditions, but the youngsters' interests were slight, and she soon began to fear this priceless heritage would be forever lost. She then chose as a goal in her life to record the beautiful Pima legends and rituals in memory of her forefathers. Her efforts resulted in her first book, *Pima Indian Legends*.

Anna fully realizes that change is inevitable. However, she has found that by stressing cultural roots as a basis for creative expression, she has been able to function constructively without having to sacrifice her culture on the altar of withdrawal or assimilation.

Acknowledgments

I HUMBLY EXPRESS MY GRATEFUL THANKS to the following people, who unselfishly gave their time and efforts toward making the dream of this book come to pass: my former teacher Anna P. Kopta; my former pastor Dr. Roe Blaine Lewis; my friend and typist Winifred Robb; photographers Robert Nuss and Helga Teiwes-French; anthropologists Edward Spicer, Bernard Fontana, and Dean and Lucille Saxton; Bert Fireman of the Arizona Historical Society; Lillian Stoffel of our basket-weaving class; and Marshall Townsend and Karen Thure of the University of Arizona Press.

In addition, many other wonderful people have provided encouragement and inspiration to me throughout my Pima past. To each of them I extend my heartfelt thanks and love.

A.M.S.

Background:
A Glimpse Into the Past

ARCHAEOLOGY REVEALS that around the year 300 B.C. a group of Indian people migrated to the Gila River Valley of Arizona. They settled near the ever-flowing Gila, which shimmered and meandered through the dry desert land. They were farmers and found ways and means to irrigate their crops by diverting water from the river with an elaborate irrigation system that featured hundreds of miles of canals. Most of these canals were about ten feet deep and thirty feet wide. They were dug with wood and stone implements, and the dirt and debris were carried away in large baskets by the women.

A thriving civilization farmed the desert along the canals until around A.D. 1200, when they vanished with no trace or explanation of their disappearance. Old Pima legends say they were driven away by enemy tribes from the east.

As you glance at many areas along the Salt and Gila valleys near the junction of the two rivers, some parts of the canals are still visible. Potsherds can be found lying on top of mounds where once a proud race had its dwellings. Excavations have brought to light basketry, stone axes, seashells, grinding stones, pit houses, and ramadas that

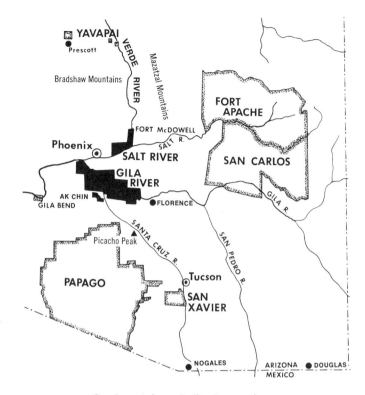

Southern Arizona Indian Reservations

attest to open-air living. From these findings, the theory has developed that the Pima and Papago tribes are descendants of these people, whom the Pimas call *Huhugam* (Those Who Are Gone). That the two tribes have common ancestors may be correct: it is true that they speak the same language with only a slight difference in the Papago dialect. Their neighboring reservations can be seen on the map on this page.

The famous Casa Grande ruins, still shrouded in mystery, were built sometime in the thirteenth century by a small ancient band called the Salado, who drifted into

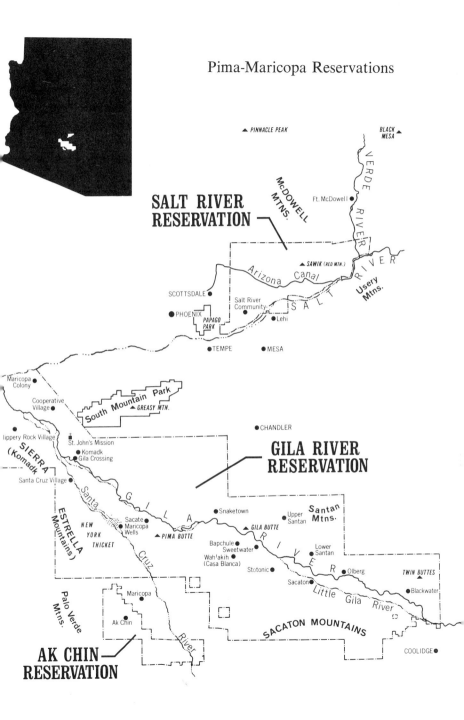

Pima-Maricopa Reservations

the region and mixed with the Huhugam. They stayed only until about 1400, then they too moved away.

According to Pima legends, *Siwani Waḻakih,* an ancient wise man, lived in the Big House. Its walls were four stories high and built from caliche that hardened like cement. Once it was surrounded by a city of considerable size. Ruins of houses are still visible around the famous Casa Grande, now a national monument. Modern generations call this amazing structure the first skyscraper.

When the first Christian missionary to the Pimas and Papagos came to the Southwest, the native Pima guides told him about the Casa Grande ruins near the Gila River. In 1694 Father Eusebio Francisco Kino rode a dusty trail to visit the Big House. What a great surprise awaited Padre Kino! The Indians were nearly naked, wearing only breech cloths, and they had long hair and tattooed faces. The gentle padre asked them, "Who built the Casa Grande?"

"Huhugam," the Pimas must have answered.

Padre Kino held mass inside the old Casa Grande walls. His joy was complete when he noticed the Pimas imitating the sign of the cross. The docile Pimas of the Gila Valley readily accepted Father Kino and his Christian teachings. They came to love him and his gentle ways.

When Padre Kino came again, he brought seeds of vegetables and fruit. These took their places among the favorite foods of the Papago, Pima, and Maricopa tribes. But the main little seed was wheat. As soon as the padre introduced it, wheat became an important part of the Indian economy. During the time of the pioneers, it saved the life of many a white tenderfoot and soldier.

Father Kino also introduced horses and cattle and helped the Indians to become better farmers. But as in the days of the Huhugam, the Gila River continued to play an important part in the lives of the natives, who were so dependent on water. Like the Nile, the Gila and Salt rivers used to overflow their banks, depositing rich loam. Men and women cooperated and went to the farms to plant seeds. A wooden *gihk,* or shovel, with a sharp end, was used to dig holes. When the tiny seed was thrown in the hole, bare heels were ready to shove the dirt over the seed.

This method of planting also was used by the Egyptians in the Nile Valley. And once a maize basket similar to those used by the Pimas was found on the island of Crete. Could it have belonged to the beautiful goddess of Pima legend, the White Clay-Eater, who left the Gila Valley to mourn for her departed twin sons and lived on an island in a distant land? The Pimas have cause to wonder if their ancestors might have wandered from Southeast Asia. Could the Pimas be the lost tribe of Israel?

After Padre Kino set his feet on the Pima desert soil, a wide door was opened for the Mexicans and Europeans. "Now the peaceful Pimas will protect us from the Apaches," they thought. Some came on foot, others on horseback and in ox carts, through southern Arizona, then a part of Mexico.

This first group of settlers had little effect on the primitive Pima way of life. It is true that many Indians now had a Spanish name as well as an Indian name, but the Pimas clung to their ancient values and legends. They continued to live in their brush round houses, called *olas kih.* People helped each other and worked together in harmony. The land belonged to everyone: a man could farm as much as he could clear and work. To keep things going smoothly, each village had a chief, who allied himself under a head chief when enemies were threatening.

In 1854 the Gadsden Purchase made southern Arizona an American territory. Now a new group of strangers came to the desert country of the Pimas: white soldiers and traders and Indian agents. The rich Pima farms provided these newcomers with food, and soon the growing Pima villages formed themselves into a pattern similar to that of today. The map in this book gives a good picture of this little string of Pima and Maricopa settlements.

Here a word should be said about the Pimas' friends, the Maricopas. Sometime in the 1700s the Maricopas fought with the other Colorado River tribes. They kept moving eastward until the middle of the nineteenth century, when they settled with the peaceful Pimas along the Gila.

But the Yumas of the Colorado River region still bore a grudge against the Maricopas. They came to Pima land to attack their old enemies in 1857. Unfortunately for them, they had not counted on the valor of the Maricopas' new allies. The Pimas and Maricopas thoroughly vanquished the Yumas, leaving almost no survivors.

After the battle, a group of Maricopas came to Pima Chief Antonio Azul and requested a small piece of land on which to build their homes. The chief went into consultation with his counselors and sub-chiefs. It was agreed that the Maricopas could live two miles west of the Sacaton Agency. But they had to promise to help the Pimas in the wars with the Apaches and other enemy tribes. Since then the Pimas and the Maricopas have been loyal allies, friends, and neighbors. They still live side by side, with the Maricopas centered on the little Ak Chin Reservation pictured on the map.

After all that roaming, one would expect the Maricopas to settle down for good. However, in 1877 a murder within the tribe caused a division. One group of dissenters moved to a spot near the junction of the Salt and Gila rivers, while another contingent joined the Mormons at their new colony of Lehi, near Mesa. The Mormons were delighted with their Indian neighbors, for they knew that they would help protect them from the marauding Apaches.

Thus it was that the Pimas, Maricopas, and Papagos helped the white man to settle the Southwest. Besides providing the newcomers with food and water, they acted as guides, soldiers, and allies to help break the threat of Apache terrorism.

Once the Apaches were conquered, the settlers were free to arrive in great numbers. Over the prairies they came, and it was not long before the old Pima way of life was deeply affected by the white man's ideas and material culture. Some of the new ways were good, and the Pimas were glad for them. Blankets, calico, and new foods, tools, and medicines made the hard lives our ancestors had lived a bit easier for us. And of course there was the Christian religion, which became so dear to the Pimas and lightened their sorrows.

But the white man brought bad things too. Liquor has broken up families, and Indian morality has conspicuously declined. Indian values have been abandoned by some of the younger generation, and they are no longer satisfied to stay at home. Many of our old arts and traditions have been lost because the white man insisted that we indiscriminately abandon all our Indian ways.

Thus as our old ones have died off the arts of cloth-weaving and pottery-making have gone with them. Our children are no longer interested in the ancient legends and ceremonies and songs, so many of these treasures have been lost forever. Diseases which the Pima had never known before came with the white man; tuberculosis struck down many of us because the Indian agents insisted that we live in poorly ventilated adobe houses instead of our airy olas kih. Many of our rich farms along the Gila and Salt rivers, which supported our ancestors for centuries, have become dry and deserted as the white man has taken the water for his own purposes.

But now we old ones are seeing the completing of the circle. Instead of insisting that we abandon our Indian ways, the white man now asks us to try to recapture our rich culture before it has completely passed away. I am telling the children on the reservation about the Huhugam; I teach them the Pima language and legends. We women get together to weave baskets in the old designs, and we have started a museum where everyone can see the beautiful artifacts of our proud Pima-Maricopa heritage.

But we can never go back to the old way of life. The white man and his cities surround us — we must embrace those of his ways which are good while keeping our pride in being Indians. The story which follows is the tale of how one family moved from the traditional way of life into the world of the white man and back to the reservation in a blending of the two. It could be the story of any Indian family.

May we go into the past and listen to the ancient Pima voices of the desert.

A Battle and a Birth

HIKWIG (WOODPECKER)* and his brother *Komkjed* (Turtle), sons of Gray Owl and his wife Red Flowers, were dancing and feasting with their families and friends. It was early autumn, the time of *S-oam Mashath,* the Yellow Moon festival, and the Pimas of the Gila River had much to celebrate. Again their fertile farms had produced a bountiful harvest of beans, corn, melons, squash, and wheat. They had invited their neighbors from the Salt River to join them in their rejoicing.

But as the merry Pimas danced and sang, they were unaware of the destiny that was in store for them. At this moment Yuma Chief Hawk Swallow and his band of warriors were trudging across the desert toward Pima land. "So the Maricopas think that they are safe with the Pimas!" the warriors murmured. "We will show that the flimsy bows and arrows of those River People are no match for our long lances, wooden clubs, and sharp knives!"

The chief's young son had accompanied his father to attain glory and experience, as was the goal of all young

---

*Woodpecker was author Anna Moore Shaw's grandfather. His son Red Arrow was her father.

boys. The warriors had gaily painted their faces and bodies. Bunched up feathers were hanging from their hair; they carried long sharp lances decorated with paint; wooden clubs hung on their belts.

The chief counselor was opposed to the attack on the Pimas and Maricopas. He advised the chief of the Yumas to abandon his plan, but Hawk Swallow insisted: "No, we are on our way to Pima land."

An Apache warrior who had joined the Yumas explained, "Let us wait and attack at night when the Pimas are asleep. Pimas do not give up easily; they fight to the end."

"No, we will go on and fight these Indians in the light of day," said the chief. "We are not cowards. Our long lances and sharp knives will do the work better than the Pima's flimsy bows and arrows!"

*   *   *

The sun was peeping over the horizon when the band of attackers reached the Maricopa village. A group of women were on their way to gather mesquite beans, and Chief Hawk Swallow grabbed one of them. She screamed, fought, and ran quickly into the thick mesquite.

"So you Maricopas thought you were safe with the Pimas!" mocked the chief. "Just where are these allies you're so proud of? We have come to fight them!"

"They're over there!" replied the frightened woman, pointing to the direction of the nearest Pima village.

The cries of the woman were heard by a Maricopa warrior who was a fast runner. He was outside his brush house tending his baby while his wife was making tortillas for breakfast. Quickly he left the child in its mother's arms and warned, "Take the baby and run to the butte for safety! The Yumas are here to fight us and our friends! I must run and tell the Pimas!"

Before long, all the villages along the Gila River were alerted. Many Pima braves rallied from as far east as Blackwater and Sacaton. Woodpecker and Turtle came from the nearby village of Sacate. When they heard the alarm they put on their war paint and picked up their heavy clubs, bows and arrows, and little round leather war shields. Together they galloped to the Maricopa Colony, where the Yumas awaited them.

A well-planned strategy was used, even though the Yumas had been allowed to draw the line for the battle. The Pimas and Maricopas stood on one side of the line, while the Yumas stood on the other. As was traditional, the warriors challenged each other to hand-to-hand combat. Woodpecker and his brother agilely dodged the lances of the Yumas and protected themselves with their shields. Their clubs and bows and arrows killed many of the enemy.

In the din of the battle, one Pima contingent kept the Yumas from going to the Gila River for a drink. Another group of Pimas stood with their backs to the sun, thereby forcing the enemy to be blinded by the bright rays. This excellent tactic was executed so quickly, it stunned the Yuma warriors. By the end of the day, almost all had been vanquished. The few wounded survivors fled to the Estrella Mountains, pursued by triumphant Pima braves. Under the cover of night, one man swam down the Gila to notify his tribe of their sad defeat.

High and safe on a butte near the river, the women and children and very old men had watched the battle. A warrior whose name was Desert Rat Tail had also climbed the butte with the females. He probably became so excited and dumbfounded at the early morning enemy surprise attack that he did not know what he was doing. It is told that he stood on the top of the butte and reported the events: "See the Yumas are burning the brush houses of the Maricopas! The angry Maricopas are now pushing the Yumas across the south side of the Gila River!"

This was too unbearable for the women. One of them said in a sneering manner, *"Ashuhya,"* an expression used only when disgusted. That was all that was said, but Desert Rat Tail took the hint and held his tongue.

In later days, when the calendar stick keepers told the story of the Yuma battle, Desert Rat Tail's cronies teased him about his day with the women. But he was good-natured and did not mind at all. Like everyone, he was proud that his tribe had so roundly defeated the Yumas in that great battle in the autumn of 1857.

*   *   *

After the Yuma battle, Woodpecker, Turtle, and the other warriors stayed away from their families for four days, until purification had taken place. The medicine men were busy whiffing tobacco, chanting, and swaying buzzard and eagle feathers to drive away any evil spirits that may have touched the warriors. Daily baths preceded the medicine men's rattling and feather-swaying. When it was certain that all was well, the men were permitted to return home for a great celebration of the victory.

How glad Woodpecker was when he saw his beloved family! His small son and daughter, *S-Kawk Pilkani* (Hard Wheat) and *Si'alig* (Dawn), were a joy to him, and his beautiful wife Yellow Leaves was expecting. The days were calm and peaceful. Winter was setting in, with the cold air turning the leaves golden.

One evening as the sun was setting, Yellow Leaves became pale from childbirth pains. Woodpecker called upon the midwife to assist her in her ordeal. Then he ran to inform his parents, Gray Owl and Red Flowers. The old ones looked alarmed, but Woodpecker reassured them. "Yes, father, I went through all the ritual purifications after the great battle."

Gray Owl sighed. "Good. We want to be certain the baby will not be touched by the evil spirits of the enemy we have just defeated."

In the *olas kih,* Yellow Leaves' pains were coming faster. Woodpecker put the children to bed: "You will see the baby in the morning."

Just as their father had promised, when Hard Wheat and Dawn awoke they saw a small baby brother. Grandmother Red Flowers helped them admire him when she came to the olas kih with unsalted green wheat gruel for Yellow Leaves. "Your mother may eat this food and grow strong," she told Dawn, "but it must never be salted. The baby's navel will not heal properly if salt is used by a mother."

*   *   *

When the baby was four days old, his godparents were sent for to give him a name. They arrived soon after the

In the old days, a family's olas kih houses were built close together, for relatives helped and protected each other. Then the white man encouraged each of us to move to a separate little plot of allotment land. Now we are scattered all over the reservation, and sometimes our own family members, especially the old people, are lonely and neglected.

news was received, and after a few words of greeting they began the christening ceremony. Time was important; evil spirits might come to the baby.

"We have decided to name your little son *S-wegi Hapot* (Red Arrow). He came to us at the most unforgettable time of the Yuma war, when many red arrows helped the Pima and Maricopa warriors win a bitter battle," said the godparents.

Then the godfather handed the baby to his godmother, who concluded the christening with her finger dipped in a mixture of water and white clay. She put a little in Red Arrow's mouth to make certain that evil spirits and lightning would not strike him as long as he lived. A small string of beads was placed around the infant's neck.

"Tomorrow you parents will present Red Arrow to the first rays of the sun," instructed the godfather, as he stood up to depart with his wife to their village of Slippery Rock in the Estrella Mountains.

Early the next morning the parents of little Red Arrow took him from his cradleboard. When the first rays of the sun appeared over the eastern hills, handsome Woodpecker proudly held his baby up to the Sun God. Beautiful Yellow Leaves stood by his side.

Woodpecker prayed: "Sun God, here is our little son Red Arrow. Let your rays fall on him. Give him a healthy body, just as your rays help our crops to grow. Let him grow and become a strong warrior to help defend his people."

The couple went into their brush house and closed the door. They were confident that their precious little son was now safe from all harm. "Go back to sleep, Yellow Leaves," her husband told her tenderly.

Caring for their children was a thing the old-time Pimas loved to do. The men shared some of the duties, including bending cradleboard frames like the one in the picture. The mothers made soft cottonwood-bark pads and willow sunshades, while the old men of the village wove little cotton blankets. How the happy babies loved to have their cradleboards rocked by the wind while a little aunt or cousin sang them a lullaby!

Woodpecker took his bow and arrows from the rafters. He knew that rabbits and quail were plentiful in the mesquite thicket. As he left he saw his dear ones sleeping, Yellow Leaves on her favorite mat and little Red Arrow in his cradleboard.

*   *   *

Before Red Arrow was born, Woodpecker had helped Yellow Leaves fashion the baby's cradleboard in the traditional way of the Pimas and Maricopas. First he had shaved the bark of the mesquite root until it was smooth. Then he slowly bent it each day until it was shaped like a large hairpin.

Yellow Leaves used the bark of an old cottonwood tree for a pad for the cradle. After she had immersed the bark in water for several days, *jewaththa* (rotting) took place. Now the rough outer bark easily separated from the long inner strands. These strands were dried in the sun, then carded, with great care taken not to break one strip. Yellow Leaves then shaped the soft cottonwood strips to form a pad for the cradleboard.

Red Arrow loved to be tied into his cradle with a beautiful hand-woven strap. This confinement was an early start at developing good sound nerves as well as obedience. The old Pimas declared truthfully that a baby would not sleep until he was strapped into his cradleboard.

Life was good for little Red Arrow. He was not only loved by his brother Hard Wheat and his sister Dawn, but his little aunts, younger sisters of his mother, often came to play with him. In this way the little Pima girls learned how to care for a baby, so that they could someday raise families of their own.

When Woodpecker moved his family from Sacate to Santa Cruz Village and set up a new cluster of olas kih homes, Red Arrow enjoyed helping haul bundles of brush to cover the dome frameworks. Yellow Leaves would smile and thank him for his tiny handfuls of sticks just as if they were as important as the huge loads of brush the adults brought to her.

Near the river, where the spring floods would bring a cover of rich mud to fertilize his crops, Woodpecker began to cultivate a new farm. There was no problem of ownership; if land was not in use, it could be worked by any Pima who so desired.

Little Red Arrow loved to watch his father plow behind his big black horse. But he liked helping his mother too. Every day he would toddle along beside her as she went about her duties of gathering wild desert foods, hauling water in her olla, and gathering wood for cooking. When he was tired, he loved to hear the stories and rules for behavior told to him by Grandfather Gray Owl and Grandmother Red Flowers. It was fun to be a Pima boy of three winters in the days of old.

A Departure for Morning Land

LONG AGO A STRANGE SICKNESS struck the Santa Cruz Village. The Pimas called it *Chuk Wihosig* (Black Vomit) because of its main symptom. A person contracting the dreadful disease would pass away in a day or two. Never in the annals of the old people had such a sickness struck down so many.

The leaders of the village believed the calamity was brought to them by some of the medicine men. "Just look at this sorrow all around us," said one of them. "The medicine men must be showing off their power again."

"They want to punish us for the disrespect shown them by the young braves," said another.

"Then let us stop the sickness by getting rid of the medicine men!" shouted the chief of the village.

Three medicine men who had been heard boasting about bringing on the Black Vomit were rounded up and slain. The sickness strangely stopped. But it did not bring back the life of little Red Arrow's mother, Yellow Leaves.

*　　*　　*

Yellow Leaves had been one of the victims of the Black Vomit. She departed for the hereafter one night when her little son Red Arrow was soundly sleeping, unaware of his mother's passing. Throughout the night he slept the peaceful sleep of childhood, while all around him busy preparations were being made for the burial.

Pima tradition did not allow a moment's waiting. Immediately after Yellow Leaves passed away she was bathed, and her long black hair was washed, brushed, and prepared as though she was going to a tribal dance. Her face was painted with a red clay called *heht;* her eyes were darkened with *mots,* a black substance used as modern girls use mascara. A string of beads was placed around her neck, and her wrists were wound with beads. Loud wailing by the mourners accompanied this work, called *ehsto* (to hide the remains).

The sad news soon spread throughout the village. But no one said the harsh words, "She has died." The Pimas' reverence for death was so great that the mourners could only say softly, "She has departed for the hereafter."

In a short time every adult in the village was awake and working to help the stricken family. Some dug a grave while others gathered Yellow Leaves' belongings — blankets, ollas, mesquite ladles, baskets, paints, and clothes — and buried them in the ground. Her pets and her horse were taken out to the desert and killed. Even her olas kih and cooking ramada were burned; nothing must remain to bring back memories of the dear departed one.

With tears in her eyes, Yellow Leaves' mother baked a small round loaf of whole wheat bread in hot ashes. This, along with a tiny olla of water and a bowl of pinole, would be placed in the grave for Yellow Leaves to eat before her departure from this world.

Pima belief about this departure was a comfort to the grieving mother. According to ancient tradition, the spirit of Yellow Leaves would hover around her home for several days, but thereafter it would take only fleeting moments to travel to the hereafter, called *Si'al Wui* (Where Morning Begins in the East). In Morning Land, Yellow Leaves would live amidst everlasting merrymaking, dancing, and Pima games of chance. It was a place where there were only happy times, the Land of the Rising Sun.

But even the thought of Morning Land did not comfort Woodpecker. He watched as his wife's remains were placed upon a handwoven cotton blanket. Tears flowed from his eyes as he and three strong friends each picked up a corner of the blanket to carry Yellow Leaves to the burial place. A wailing, chanting crowd formed a procession behind them.

"Ni-mad! (my daughter!)" cried her mother, over and over in mournful song. The men also cried aloud. No one was ashamed to weep for the departed one, their beloved, their sacrificed one.

At the burial ground, the grave had been made ready. Now a small cave was dug on one side of the pit. Into this cave went Yellow Leaves' favorite woven sleeping mat, her blanket, her soft homemade pillow filled with brown tops of cattails, and the food her mother had prepared. Dry cactus ribs were stuck in the ground around the crypt, and it was covered with a blanket to keep the loose dirt from falling on the body. Men took turns at covering the grave with Mother Earth. Last came the spreading of thorny mesquite branches and the laying on of long, heavy posts to keep the wind from uncovering the grave. There

This picture of the Sacaton cemetery was taken around the turn of the century. Yellow Leaves was buried in such an unmarked grave. Now we have beautiful stone monuments for our departed loved ones, but the grief we feel is no greater than that of the Pimas of old.

was nothing else to be done. The earthly remains of Yellow Leaves had been ehsto. Work was finished.

The grief-stricken family and friends wailed and sang their mourning songs while a leader stood before them and spoke words of comfort and advice. "Your loved one has gone to the Rising Sun. We will not look on her again. We must never mention her name again."

All the mourners knew that this must be so. Never could they speak the name of Yellow Leaves, for were they to do so, evil spirits might bring them sickness and death.

But this did not mean that the Pimas ceased to mourn after the burial. Even though they could not say the name of the departed, expressions of sympathy and kinship were uttered over and over again. The mourners wore sackcloth for a month. Widows and widowers mourned for a whole year and could not marry again during that time, or the new mate would meet the same fate as their former one.

The male never cut his matted strips of hair, but a widow had to cut her long black hair up to her earlobes. In the days before scissors, this had to be done by singeing, and the smell of burning hair came to be associated with death.

In addition to her short hair, a widow was distinguished by her clothes. She could not wear a dress but wrapped a blanket around her body up to her armpits, leaving her arms bare. She must not have any social life or she would be the topic of the village gossip.

*   *   *

These traditions were repeated to Woodpecker by his aged parents, Gray Owl and Red Flowers, who sat weep-ing beside him. Little Red Arrow looked up at his father in bewilderment and asked, *"Ni-mahm* (my father), where is *ni-tha'al* (my mother)?"

His father did not hear Red Arrow. No one paid any attention to the little boy who had slept soundly and did not yet know of his mother's passing. All were absorbed in their own sorrow.

"I know — she is over at the well!" cried Red Arrow. The well was quite a distance away, near a running brook. Many a time Red Arrow had walked there, hand-in-hand with his mother, her olla perched on her head. He had always felt so secure with his mother there beside him.

Yellow Leaves would fill her olla with water while the little boy watched his friend the dragonfly skim gracefully on the water's surface and the playful tadpole swim in the brook. How Red Arrow had screamed and laughed watching the little tadpoles!

When the boy finally arrived at the spring, he shouted, "Ni-tha'al! Ni-tha'al!" But there was no answer. He sat on the bank of the brook and cried louder. Where could his mother be?

In the distance a hungry coyote heard the child's cries and came running. Red Arrow had often been warned by his mother, "The coyote is always hungry; run for your life if ever a coyote comes!" The lad remembered this advice and hurried away from the coyote, crying loudly in fear. He ran behind a large bush, and the coyote slowly chased him around it.

At that moment a young Pima maiden was on her way to the well. When she heard Red Arrow's cries of fear, she hurriedly left her olla beside the trail and ran to the well in time to save the child from the coyote's sharp fangs.

Loudly she shouted an old Pima expression: *"Huah! Huah! Si woho ap hig!"* The sly old coyote slunk away into the thicket.

"G wo i hihim (come), Red Arrow; I will take you home," said the maiden softly. She dried the little boy's tears and started for the village, carrying him on her back. They had not gone far when Grandmother Red Flowers met them. She cried when she saw her little grandson looking so lonely and frightened.

The maiden told her how little Red Arrow had been chased around a big bush by a coyote. The two women cried together, for they knew that Red Arrow would have been eaten by the hungry animal.

Red Flowers took the maiden's hand and said, "My grandniece" four times, in the old Pima tradition. The maiden repeated "My grandaunt" four times, then started down the trail to pick up her olla.

Red Flowers placed her little grandson on her back and returned to the village. Woodpecker saw them from a distance and ran to help his mother. He carried the now-sleeping lad into the olas kih. Gently he laid him on his grass mat.

Grandmother told of the near-tragedy with the coyote. "We must watch Red Arrow well from now on. He is still a baby!" cried Woodpecker, sobbing aloud.

When little Red Arrow awoke he asked again, "Ni-mahm, where is ni-tha'al?" Woodpecker gathered his son in his arms and with tears freely flowing down his face told Red Arrow in simple words: "My son, your mother went to Si'al Wui, where the sun comes up. Red Arrow, you must never call your mother from now on. Bad spirits and bad dreams will make you sick."

It was difficult for a child as young as Red Arrow to understand, but he knew he must obey his mahm. He tried very hard not to speak of his mother again, but her warmth and beauty remained in his thoughts for many winters.

Childhood's Happy Times

LIFE WOULD HAVE BEEN HARD for Woodpecker if his parents had not given him their assistance, but in the old days families helped each other. Red Flowers naturally assumed responsibility for the education of Hard Wheat, Dawn, and little Red Arrow. "There must be no questionable whisperings about my grandchildren," she told Woodpecker. "It is my task to see that they grow up in the right way."

Under her grandmother's teaching, little Dawn soon learned to help with the household chores. How often she heard the words, "Do not gad about the village like a hungry burro! Stay home and help your grandmother with the cooking." This advice readied her for marriage, for preparing food was an important part of a Pima woman's work. "Stay home and have the meals ready for your husband," Grandmother Red Flowers would tell her time and time again. "Never keep him waiting. Keep your bean pot full of something to eat. Never be lazy. No one wants a lazy wife."

After a day of gathering wild foods, hauling water and wood, grinding corn, and cooking, Dawn would be tired. Then she would join the family on mats around the fire

A woman's *gioho* (burden basket) was beautifully crocheted of mescal-fiber string; in fact it looked just like a fine lace tablecloth. But these baskets, which were really more like nets, were tough enough to carry one hundred pounds of wood or wild foods. The women who used them were tough, too — they often ran along with their heavy loads as if they were light as straw!

to hear stories and receive still more advice on becoming a wise and good woman.

"Do not gad about the homes; winds will carry your name all over. You will give your parents a bad name if you are known as a village gossip."

"When the Pimas are on the warpath, do not marry a foe's son."

"Respect your elders and obey them."

"Do not be *s-chu tha'a* (selfish). Show your kindness to your visitors by providing them with pinole. Then get busy and cook a meal for them."

"Pay attention and learn to weave baskets in the old manner. This will teach you patience, and you will not be lazy. Give your first woven basket to an expert basket-weaver. Some of her skill then will rub off on you."

"If a hen should crow like a rooster, it is a bad sign. The hen should be killed to stop evil spirits from bringing harm to you and your family."

"Do not step on snake marks in the road; otherwise you will marry a snake."

Hard Wheat and Red Arrow received advice too. Woodpecker and Gray Owl would tell them, "Sons, do not form the habit of borrowing. Things borrowed never last. Work for the horse and the cow that you need."

"Do not steal your brother's or friend's wife. Hearts will become *si-wihonagi* (ruffled) and *siw* (bitter)."

"Evil spirits will take away your strength if you marry a girl from an enemy camp. You will become a weakling."

"Never eat your first kill, whether it be a dove, a cottontail, or a quail. If you do so you will have bad luck and never attain skill in hunting. It is better to give your first kill to an old man who was once an expert hunter. Then some of his skill will rub off on you."

"The hooting of an owl is a bad omen: it is the voice of the deceased returning to tell of a coming catastrophe. In war, however, you should give the owl hoot as a sign to warn of enemy warriors hiding in the thicket."

"Cling to your land. Do not sell it. Land will last. After you are gone it will still be here for the future Pima generations. It would be a sad thing to deny land to our sons."

Even when Red Arrow was just a toddler running about in a little cotton shirt that fell to his knees, he heard this advice repeated to him. As he grew older and began to wear a breech cloth, he came to understand the words more and more and to bear them firmly in his mind.

But always Red Arrow's favorite advice was the kind that came through the old legends. He would smile in anticipation when his grandfather started to tell one of the many old tales, such as the story of *Tahmog,* the Milky Way.

"A long, long time ago," Gray Owl would begin, "when the world was new, *Ban* (Coyote) stole an old woman's *chu'i* (pinole). The chief of the village chased the thief. To escape, Ban flew to the sky, spilling the white chu'i across it. The chief flew after him. When he caught the culprit, he angrily picked him up and flung him to the moon.

"Thus, on a bright moonlit night, the desert coyotes look up to the sky. They see the coyote in the moon and wail for their brother. And when you look up at the sky, Red Arrow, you can still see the pinole, scattered all across it."

After a pause, Grandmother Red Flowers would warn the children: "See the naughty, naughty coyote up in the moon? He's a prisoner there because he stole the old woman's pinole. Do not steal. It is very wrong."

*   *   *

Besides learning proper behavior, Hard Wheat and Red Arrow had to learn to hunt game for Dawn's ever-simmering cooking pot. By the time they were nine years old they were expected to be skilled enough with their bows and arrows to bring home small birds and animals. Sometimes the boys of the village would go together on a rabbit drive, and their excited shouts could be heard in the thickets and desert all around the village.

Red Arrow especially liked to hunt eagles for pets. After he had captured one of the great birds, he would proudly wear the feathers in his hair.

It was important that Pima boys become good runners. This helped them in hunting and in battle, and it made them strong. As soon as they were free from work the children would go out to the desert to run races. Sometimes their older relatives would come along to cheer for them and give them advice.

One evening as they sat by the fire, Woodpecker prepared his sons for more discipline of the body. "It is important for every Pima boy to take a plunge in the cold water before the sun comes up over the hills. This will harden you and prepare you to become strong warriors. It will also keep away the evil spirits."

So it was that the next morning at dawn Woodpecker awakened the boys. "Get up, Hard Wheat and Red Arrow — this is the day you will go to the ditch for a dip!"

The sleepy boys wanted to stay on their cozy grass mats, but they had to obey their father. They raced to the nearby ditch, jumped into the cold water and out again, then ran back to the olas kih.

How good it felt to warm themselves near the blazing fire on the dirt floor! Grandmother Red Flowers had prepared hot green wheat gruel. As they greedily ate the nourishing food, Woodpecker spoke to the shivering boys: "Now, my sons, the evil spirit will not come near you. You will be hardened, brave warriors."

*　　*　　*

Red Arrow thought it was much more fun to swim with his friends in the deep, cool pools of the flowing Gila River. How refreshing this was on a summer day when the desert shimmered in the heat! The swimmers would climb trees like cats, then jump into the water, shouting and splashing in good-natured fun.

But for most of the day in the summer, Red Arrow was with his father in the fields. Here he learned to cultivate the land, to sow seeds, and irrigate his crops. Everyone in the village was a farmer, and it was important for Red Arrow to learn the skills so he could feed a family of his own someday.

Sometimes there was a tribal dance or celebration. Then there was no work; the children could play all day, watch dancing and sporting events, and feast on special foods. Often the people of another village would come to share the festivities at Santa Cruz, and the boys and girls could make new friends.

But Red Arrow did not need festivals to be happy, for even day-to-day work was fun for this hardy Pima boy.

He liked his busy hours of hunting and farming and playing with his friends. At night his grandparents' stories and legends were fascinating. Even though he had lost his mother at an early age, Red Arrow grew up strong and healthy, his days filled with childhood's happy times.

The Making of a Warrior

EARLY ONE MORNING, Woodpecker rolled out of his woven yucca mat. His face was lined with worry and fatigue. He had spent a sleepless night because of a decision concerning Red Arrow.

As a devoted father, he had made sure that Red Arrow learned everything important to attaining noble Pima manhood. But there was one skill he had put off teaching his son. Now Red Arrow was twelve years old, and Gray Owl was asking, "My son Woodpecker, when are you going to have Red Arrow trained in the use of the shield? The longer you delay, the harder it will be for the boy to become skilled in the art of battle."

Finally at dawn, Woodpecker made his decision: "I am grieved at the thought of losing my precious son to the enemy. But I must be strong. I cannot put off Red Arrow's shield training any longer. My son must begin his preparation for the war trails."

Woodpecker walked slowly to his parents' nearby olas kih. His father was crawling on hands and knees through the low doorway. In the stiff manner of the aged, he stood up. His son spoke to him: "Ni-mahm, I must talk to you. It is about Red Arrow."

"Good," said Gray Owl, dusting the dirt from his bare knees.

"Father, I have decided to begin Red Arrow's shield training. Could you mend my old shield for him? He'll need it to practice with until a new one is made."

"Woodpecker, my son, I've made a new one. The old one is not good enough for my grandson. It takes many moons to become skillful with the *kawad*."

Just then, Red Arrow galloped by on his pony Buckskin, on his way back from watering the horses at the Gila River. He heard his father calling from the ramada, "Red Arrow, I want to talk to you!"

Red Arrow alighted from his pony and obediently walked to where his father was waiting for him. "Yes ni-mahm," he answered, standing tall and straight as an arrow. The boy's long black hair hung loosely around his shoulders, and he wore a red headband to keep his hair from his eyes. His red breech cloth disclosed his bare legs, which resembled the smooth limbs of a swift antelope. On his feet he wore cowhide sandals.

"Yes, father," repeated Red Arrow. But his father was too absorbed in his thoughts to hear him: "If only this boy's mother were here beside me!"

Again Red Arrow made his presence known.

"Yes, yes, son," answered Woodpecker, as his mind came back to the moment at hand. "Sit down." There were no chairs in those days, so Red Arrow sat on his grandmother's wooden mortar, while his father settled on her stone metate.

Woodpecker spoke on the subject that was uppermost in his heart. "Son, it is the tradition of the Pimas to give their sons an early training in the art of war. Your Uncle Turtle will be here today to teach you the art of the kawad, the shield. Red Arrow, you must be trained in order to protect yourself and your people. You must be ready to take the place of some old warrior who will someday lay down his weapons. Are you willing?"

"Yes, father, I am willing to defend my people," said Red Arrow.

Woodpecker continued: "These days the tribes are so often at war. The Apaches come from the north to fight us. The Yumas also come from the western hills to satisfy their hearts. At the present time, some of our warriors — *Komadk Shon,* Owl Ear, Black Shirt, and many others — are scouting the Red Mountain area north of Salt River. It is safer to go after the Apaches rather than wait for their surprise attacks. My son Red Arrow, I have spoken from the depth of my heart."

Woodpecker arose to show his speech was over. He stood musing on the past, remembering how his lonely little three-year-old had longed for his mother and the time the little boy had been nearly devoured by a coyote. Once before that, Yellow Leaves had saved him from drowning. Now he would go on the war trail, and the enemy might take his life.

Woodpecker's gloomy thoughts were interrupted by Red Arrow shouting the Pima battle cry: *"Hipah! Hipah!"* The boy was fired with enthusiasm, and his shouts had burst forth spontaneously. His exuberance relieved his father's doubts and fears.

Red Arrow was jumping around, pretending to fight a foe, beating the air with his fists. "Take that and that, you

Geronimo White Hat! Ha! you don't know it, but you're giving me an exciting adventure."

"Red Arrow! Come and eat!" called his sister from the doorway of the olas kih.

The Indian boy walked slowly to the house, but he was too excited to eat. "I wish mother were here to see me use the shield!" Then he remembered he was forbidden ever to mention the departed ones, for evil spirits would bring bad dreams and even death.

"Red Arrow, you seem so far away this morning. Is it Laughing Brook, the pretty one you're thinking of?" teased Dawn.

"Hmmm," joined in Hard Wheat, "Red Arrow's going to become a famous warrior. His name should remind him to stand straight, think straight, and shoot straight."

"Hard Wheat, stop teasing your brother," said Uncle Turtle. "Red Arrow is going to walk in the footsteps of his father, who helped whip the Yumas near the Estrella Mountains."

*   *   *

Uncle Turtle had arrived at Woodpecker's olas kih soon after he heard of his brother's decision. After eating the delicious breakfast Dawn had prepared, he joined Woodpecker and Gray Owl. Together they walked to the ramada to smoke home-grown coyote tobacco, called *ban wiwga*.

Woodpecker spoke first: "Red Arrow is very fond of you, my brother Turtle. He'd rather take his training from you than from anyone else."

"I'm very fond of Red Arrow too. He'll make a good warrior like our father," said Turtle.

"Aw! you boys did well in battle too!" injected Gray Owl. "After a fight, for days it is heard about the village: 'Turtle and Woodpecker have added more enemy hair trophies to their belts.' "

Turtle stood up and called, "Red Arrow, come! It's time to begin your shield lesson."

The Indian boy ran out of the brush house, where he had remained to help Dawn and to discuss her puberty dance, which would surely happen someday very soon.

"Take the shield and get the feel of it," advised Turtle, handing the round shield to Red Arrow.

"Yi, Yi, Yi! The animal skin is tough but very smooth; just like an olla!" exclaimed Red Arrow, running his fingers over the shield's surface.

"Yes, your Grandfather Gray Owl made it for you."

"For me?" asked Red Arrow as he proudly hugged the little shield.

"Before we begin," said Turtle, "I want to stress the importance of this little round thing we call a shield. It is a shield, a protector of lives, in every sense of the word. The skillful use of it has saved many a Pima from certain death."

The young lad felt very grown up. The feeling of responsibility crept into his heart, and he admired his uncle's courage and devotion. Red Arrow thought to himself, "I want to be just like Uncle Turtle."

"This little shield won many a battle for us," began Turtle. And he went on to tell a story:

"One night a young boy was irrigating his father's wheat field. A band of Apaches suddenly ambushed him. His

A brave's shield was his treasured possession and close friend. His life depended upon his ability to wield it for protection in battle. The sight of a Pima skillfully brandishing his colorful shield while threatening with his war club was enough to strike fear in the heart of any foe!

father heard his son's cries and ran to rescue him from the clutches of the enemy. The father shouted *'Ohb! Ohb!* (Apache! Apache!).'

"The Pimas heard the warning. The mothers hushed the cries of their children, and the warriors seized their weapons and went forth to defend their homes.

"Sun Rays, a young lad, was given the task of spreading the news of attack to the villages along the upper Gila Valley. He jumped on his horse and rode bareback, shouting 'Ohb! Ohb!' to warn the people in the Blackwater area.

"Before long, there was a cloud of dust; hoofbeats of horses and war whoops of angry Pimas filled the night air. Antonio Azul, chief of the Pimas, led the Sacaton warriors to help us. They were like a swarm of·hornets ready to retaliate.

"When the Apaches heard the loud commotion, they ran back to their hilly country. Their leader Geronimo was very crafty and knew when to fight.

"Chief Azul led us to Crooked [Superstition] Peak, the Apaches' hideout in the Superstition Range. There we spent considerable time searching for the enemy's tracks. We saw not a trace of them. Apaches are clever; also agile climbers.

"The sun was going by very quickly when we climbed the rugged mountain. We stumbled over jagged rocks and thorny cacti. With eyes swollen and bruised bodies, we were ready to drop from exhaustion. But our instincts told us not to give up. So we continued climbing the slopes of Crooked Mountain.

"Rain Cloud, a Gila Crossing scout, gave owl hoots to signal us to move cautiously. 'Look at the tiny trail of smoke curling up from the canyon,' he whispered. 'See the Ohb walking around the campfire?'

"A council was held on the rim of the canyon. Our case looked hopeless, for the ravine had steep walls of rock. We figured the Apaches must have a secret trail to their camp. To go down in the hole would be sure death, like going into a trap. Ah! those clever Apaches!

"Chief Azul decided against going into the gully. 'We must not jeopardize the lives of our warriors.'

"*Sthahiwuim* [Walks Like He Is Ready to Sit Down], a Gila Crossing warrior, displayed courage, and by that I mean *real* courage — he spoke against the decision of the great Chief Azul. 'Nothing is stopping us!' said Sthahiwuim. 'We're going into the pit to fight! We've come this far; we can't give up now! Come, Gila Crossing braves, let's go!'

"Sthahiwuim took his shield and placed it on the edge of the precipice, muttering, 'Our gods will help us!' He sat on his shield, with his weapons on his back, and went sliding down the smooth canyon walls. He used his hands to guide and break his fall.

"The words of Sthahiwuim placed courage in our hearts to follow him all the way, even if it meant death. So together we went sliding on our shields. After we landed at the bottom of the canyon, we surrounded the Apache from every side. We yelled our war cries, '*Haia, haia Ohb!*' The stunned Apaches gave no resistance. Our shouts echoed in the canyon like the loud clapping of thunder on a summer day."

At this point of the story, Turtle's hands waved and gestured in emotion. The bitterness of long ago flashed across his battle-scarred face. The tense muscles on his neck stood out conspicuously. Panting hard, he blurted thickly, "I do not need to say who won the battle!"

Wiping the beads of sweat from his face, Turtle resumed his talk. "This is how important the shield is. It went through sweat and blood with us. Red Arrow, don't ever forget!"

The face of Red Arrow was pale. His body felt weak and numb, but he managed to reply fervently, "Uncle Turtle, I'll never forget it as long as I live!"

"Good," said Uncle Turtle. "Handle your shield like you would fragile pottery. Hang it where careless hands and hungry dogs will not touch it."

"I will," promised Red Arrow.

"Then shall we begin with the shield lesson?" asked Uncle Turtle. "I will show you. The first thing is to hold the shield in front of you at all times. Crouch low. Hold it so your eyes will just barely see over the rim, so you can watch every movement of your opponent. Leap from side to side in a zigzag manner. At the same time advance toward your opponent. A slight twist of your forearm will revolve the shield. Its brilliant colors will confuse and frighten the enemy. Apaches are afraid of evil spirits too. At the first careless move your foe makes, rush to him and end the fight with your war club. You save your arrows by this close combat method."

"Tomorrow we'll begin, using mudballs instead of real arrows. Your brother Hard Wheat will be your opponent. Red Arrow, any questions?"

"Yes, Uncle Turtle, were you ever scared of the Apaches?"

Turtle smiled. "Just like a boy to ask such a question,"

he thought. He answered, "Yes, many a time, but only at the starting point. A warrior must be brave and die with a silent throat."

*   *   *

Every day from then on there was shield practice for Red Arrow. Uncle Turtle had his own way of training. He was strict with his nephew because he was so late in attaining the skill. The young lad was eager to learn so he would be able to protect himself and his people from the foe's swift arrows. He took to heart his uncle's often-repeated words: "The art of war needs strength, alertness, and skill. It is hard work. One must practice every day if he is to survive the cruelty of war."

First came many weeks of practice with mudballs instead of arrows. More often than not the mudballs hit Red Arrow's body, for he had not yet learned to stop them with his shield. Finally one day Uncle Turtle announced, "Today we are going to use real arrows instead of mud. You can do it Red Arrow," he encouraged, when he saw his nephew's frightened face.

Hard Wheat knew how Red Arrow must feel deep inside his being. He had had the same experience at his first training. "Uncle Turtle is a strict trainer," he thought. "I will be very careful not to hurt my little brother."

"Boys, let us begin," commanded Turtle. The brothers stood quite a distance from each other, their weapons in readiness for a real hand-to-hand fight. Hard Wheat clutched his bow and arrow in his right hand, while Red Arrow had his war club hanging on his belt and his round shield in his left hand. "It is good you are left-handed, Red Arrow," said Turtle. "You will quickly confuse the enemy because they are superstitious and afraid of left-handed foes."

When they were ready, Turtle shouted from the side lines, *"Thohwa'i!* (Ready, go!) Now you are enemies! Fight for your lives!"

The brothers went through their parts, breathing hard, perspiration pouring down their bodies. *"A-yuh! Aik-honih!"* Red Arrow shouted old Pima exclamations when he saw the arrows flying in his direction. It was all he could do to block the arrows with his shield and leap sideways in a zigzag manner, using the round shield for protection.

"Remember — you are enemies and fighting for your very lives! You are too slow, Red Arrow! Do not drag your feet, or the enemy will shoot your legs off," warned Uncle Turtle.

Red Arrow was awkward with his feet, for it was hard to crouch and at the same time leap from side to side. But his trainer was demanding, always shouting new instructions: "Stay low, close to the ground. That's the way! Make your steps toward your enemy. Now twirl your shield to frighten and confuse him!"

After a few more rounds, Turtle decided it was time to stop. It wouldn't be right to exhaust Red Arrow in his first real practice. "Sit down, boys," he said. "I want to speak to you."

"Red Arrow, if you are ever shot in a real battle, you must pull out the arrow shaft, even if the pain is great.

Then crawl into a cave or thicket to rest. The good pinole in the little bag on your belt and the water in your gourd canteen will help you to regain your strength.

"When you kill an enemy in battle, do not take it lightly. It is a victory, but nonetheless, taking a life makes unpleasant and never-forgotten memories. This is why all Pima warriors must go through the purification ceremonies after a battle.

"But enough of words. Red Arrow, you have shown skill with the kawad. Hard Wheat, you did well too. This will be all for today. Boys, run to the river and wash your bodies."

"I'll race you, Red Arrow!" shouted Hard Wheat, and the brothers raced to the river to splash and play. A group of boys were waiting at the swimming hole. "Red Arrow and Hard Wheat, let's play warriors on the war trail!"

Opposing teams were chosen, with Red Arrow and Gray Fox as leaders. Mud images were slapped into place and lined up facing each other. The teams waited for the word ready — *thohwa'i!* Mudballs representing arrows were thrown at the images. The game ended as Gray Fox's team lost all of their warriors. "Haia Ohb!" laughed the boys.

*   *   *

As Red Arrow rested under the shade of a cottonwood tree, he thought about the events of the morning. Mudball battles were fun, but today he had faced real arrows. He was on his way to becoming a real warrior. He remembered the words of his Uncle Turtle: "A warrior must be brave and die with a silent throat." He hoped he could be truly brave in defense of his people.

The Threshold of Womanhood

DAWN HAD COME A LONG WAY from the scared six-year-old
who had cried in the night as she heard strange grown-up
voices chanting her mother's mourning songs. Now she
was a tall and dignified young maiden, modest and hard-
working as well as darkly beautiful.

Training for womanhood under the watchful tutelage of
Grandmother Red Flowers had not been easy. As a mother
grows old, her legs become tired, and the daughter must
help with the cooking. But when one has only a grandmother, the girl must do much more, for the old one's legs
are infirm and wobbly, unable to perform the many heavy
chores required of a Pima woman.

Since the time of her mother's death, Dawn had arisen
each day before sunrise to grind corn or wheat on the stone
metate. At first, as an awkward child, it had been hard to
grind the grain fine enough to be easily kneaded into the
soft *chemait* (bread) Grandfather Gray Owl loved. But
now that the girl was grown, her grinding was rhythmic
and easy, a beautiful way to begin each day.

After the grinding and preparing the morning meal,
Dawn always took a walk to a bubbling spring near the
Gila River. Confidently and with grace, the maiden walked

National Anthropologist Archives, Smithsonian Institution

To me one of the best symbols of old-time Pima life is a woman grinding corn or wheat on her worn stone metate. We children used to gather around our mothers and grandmothers as they worked, for they would tell us stories. They made the grinding seem so easy; not until my mother tried to teach me the skill did I learn about sore knees and tired muscles!

home each day with her heavy, water-filled olla balanced on a padded ring upon her head. Quail crossed her path, and rabbits played in the desert growth as the sun began to shed its warmth on the little Pima settlement.

Placing her olla in the ramada's shade, Dawn would begin the task of washing little brown tepary beans for her clay bean pot. After making a fire of just the right temperature, she would put the pot on the coals to simmer. Now the beans could take care of themselves, for when the sun was directly overhead, hungry men would return to the olas kih, anxious for pinole, cool water, and a rest before returning to the fields for the afternoon's labor.

In the evening, when the sun was setting red and gold, Dawn's simmering beans would finally be soft and delicious, ready for the major hardy meal of the old-time Pima day.

Gathering the wild desert foods was another of Dawn's chores. Sometimes this seemed hard, but more often the girl and her friends would make a holiday of it. Dawn especially loved to dig for the tiny potato-like nodules called *ihkow*. When she had collected sufficient amounts of these delicacies, she would take them home to boil in her bean pot. How her little brother Red Arrow loved the ihkow! He thought they tasted like the sugar cubes Woodpecker sometimes brought him from the store at *Wah'akih* (Casa Blanca).

* * *

At night, when the family lay full and happy about the fire, Dawn would feel pride in her gathering and cooking. Feeding a family was a satisfying and rewarding experi-

ence — yet not enough to entirely fulfill a bright and creative young girl. Dawn's life did not become complete until
the day dear Grandmother Red Flowers decided that her
young fingers had reached the stage where they could learn
to weave the magnificent Pima baskets.

Dawn helped gather river willow twigs and cattail reeds
with eager glee. She gladly picked the black devil's claws
at the edges of the irrigated fields, for these weeds would
form the striking black designs on her beautiful baskets.
Red Flowers showed her granddaughter how to place the
devil's claws in water for a week, to soften the tough thorns.
After the two had stripped the sides of each claw with
sharp awls, they threw the rest of the plant away.

Next came preparation of the cattails. Red Flowers
demonstrated the trick of splitting the weeds with the teeth,
then spreading them in the sun to dry. The young willow
twigs were stripped free of leaves, then split in half with
the teeth. These were rolled up while damp and flexible,
then tied with string or strips of willow bark and hung on
the rafters of the olas kih to dry until they were needed.

At first it was hard for Dawn's untrained fingers to learn
the complex art. "Have patience, my dear," grandmother
would say. "Basket-weaving is to teach you patience, my
granddaughter."

But it took such infinite patience! To weave intently,
then unravel when it was not perfect, was the hardest
thing for Dawn. But in time her fingers grew supple and
skillful. When Grandmother Red Flowers finally nodded
with prideful approval upon seeing a finished basket, Dawn
knew she was ready to go to *Nahsa,* the famous weaver,
who lived in Slippery Rock Village.

Besides their famous smaller baskets covered with beautiful designs, Pima basket-weavers made coiled storage bins of straw. After the harvest, these huge baskets held mesquite beans, corn, and wheat to eat during the winter famine.

"Please, grandmother," Dawn said humbly. "I would like to learn the art from the great Nahsa."

"You are ready, my child," replied grandmother with love, "but you know you must stay with her for one whole moon in order to learn properly. Are you ready to leave us for such a time, Dawn?"

Dawn looked up at her grandmother respectfully. "I wish to learn to weave, grandmother," she said simply. "I wish to become expert like the great Nahsa."

So it was that Red Flowers took Dawn to Nahsa. The old lady lived in an olas kih of her son's household and spent all her days weaving the most beautiful of baskets. She was an exacting but patient teacher. How many times she said softly, "No, Dawn, the devil's claw goes this way in this design — in a circle, not an oval. This is the ancient maze pattern of Pima legend. You must make it right, Dawn, exactly right."

After one month of weaving, Dawn's basket was perfect. The traditional Pima patterns of long ago marched along the sides of it in beautiful symmetry. When Red Flowers came to get her granddaughter she marveled at the work. She said nothing, but in truth she could not tell this basket from one of Nahsa's.

Dawn wanted to keep her masterpiece, but for years she had been told that she must give her first great finished basket to her teacher for good luck. In this way, Nahsa's talent would rub off on her, and in her time she would gain the skill and renown of an expert.

*   *   *

Gray Owl, Woodpecker, and her two brothers never saw Dawn's first great weaving achievement. But the obvious pride of Grandmother Red Flowers was enough for the young girl. She was settled back at home and beginning a basket on her own when a strange thing happened. "All is not right with me; something is wrong now," thought the maiden. At first she was embarrassed to tell her grandmother, but when the trouble continued, she was forced to confess.

"Grandmother, I am so ashamed to tell you."

"What is it, my child?" asked Red Flowers softly.

"Grandmother, I am discharging blood," moaned the girl, almost in tears.

Red Flowers smiled and put her arms around Dawn. "Child, do not be ashamed. I went through the same thing, as do all young Pima girls. Now, however, you must go to the olas kih yonder, where no one lives. Here you must stay isolated for seven days, or the medicine man will put a curse on you. If you do not remain there, bad spirits will hover over you, and you will get sick and die."

Dawn's brow was knitted, and her face showed fear.

"My dear child," repeated her grandmother. "All is well. This is a time for rejoicing, not crying. Dawn, you will soon become a woman."

When her seven days of isolation were over, Dawn was taken to the Santa Cruz, where Red Flowers bathed her and washed her long black hair. As they returned to the family olas kih, the grandmother told her granddaughter of the preparations which were already underway for a great puberty dance.

"So this is what it is about!" thought Dawn. "I will soon be a woman, with a family of my own. But first will come my wonderful dance!"

Everyone in Red Arrow's olas kih was busy making

preparations for Dawn's puberty festival. Red Flowers had to supervise the preparation of a great feast. Gray Owl took it upon himself to make sandals of soft buckskin for his granddaughter to wear. He also shaved long sticks smooth and decorated them with eagle feathers for Dawn to carry.

Before the white man came, a girl's puberty costume was made entirely from natural materials, but now that there was a trading post at Casa Blanca, blooming girls like Dawn could be arrayed in bright printed calico and beads of red, white, and blue, all traded for laboriously cultivated Indian wheat.

*   *   *

When the great day came, Dawn was dressed in a new white muslin shirt with short sleeves. Then came a yard of red calico, the hard-won beads and matching earrings, and the exquisite handmade sandals. Dawn's clean, glossy black hair was touched here and there with wet white clay. The fine black clay called mots enhanced her large brown eyes. Tall and magnificent, with high cheeks blushing pink and dark eyes glowing, Dawn was one of the most beautiful girls the Pimas had ever seen.

Now came the night of her glory. The traditional feast was savory and rich, and Dawn was the center of attention in the special dance called *E'eda i Wohp* (Middle Run), similar to the white man's Virginia Reel. Dawn's part was to lag behind all the dancers, to be seen and pointed out as the honored one. Next came the round dance, in which all could participate. When the ring of revelers became too large, another and yet another ring was formed. The earth resounded and trembled with music and thumping Pima feet.

When all had ended and morning had come, Dawn awoke, half-dreaming. Many a young brave had admired her the night before, and the girl knew that some of them would ask Woodpecker for her hand in marriage. Whom would he choose? *Tash Bijim* (Sundown) was nice, but *Ha-a Hainig* (Broken Olla) was so good-looking and hard-working.

Grandmother Red Flowers interrupted Dawn's day-dreams. "My child, your Aunt *Kalnih Saw* has come to tattoo your lower eyelids and the corners of your lower lip. This is the final part of the puberty rite. After this last pain, you will be a woman."

"Grandmother, do I have to? I am tired, and it will hurt, I know."

"If you refuse to be tattooed, all the women of the village will scorn you and call you *Hohhi Wuhpi* (Dove Eyes, Reddish Eyes)."

Dawn sighed. "I will be brave and go through the ordeal. No one shall call me Dove Eyes."

Aunt Kalnih Saw was tender, but still the pain seemed great. She used the hard, sharp thorns of a small tree called *uhs chewadpad,* the white man's crucifixion thorn, a native of the Southwestern desert. Dawn gritted her teeth and did not cry out, but it took four days of isolation on her pallet for her to recover from the ordeal.

When all was healed, and Dawn's eyes and mouth were properly enhanced according to tribal custom, she was thrilled to see the handsome brave Broken Olla approaching her home. So this was the man Woodpecker had chosen!

Dawn's new husband spent four nights with her in the family olas kih. After this, according to the old tradition, the two were legally married. Now it was time for Dawn, for so long the mainstay of her father's household, to leave with her husband for his home. Upon her arrival, her mother-in-law would leave wheat beside the metate for her to grind to prove her industry. But that would be no problem for Woodpecker's daughter, who had helped cook for a household since the age of six!

Broken Olla was strong and brave. Only his firm warm hand in hers gave Dawn the strength to leave the familiar home she had kept for so many years.

"Goodbye, grandfather. Farewell, father. And my dear brothers, I will visit you often." Dawn was almost in tears as she turned to Grandmother Red Flowers.

The wise old one took the girl's hand in hers. "Dawn, you are grown now," she said. "You must begin your own family soon."

"Yes, grandmother, but how will you manage?"

"The boys are growing fast, my child. In no time they will bring home brides of their own to help us with our work. Now go and be a good wife. Do not worry about us, Dawn."

The bridegroom and his bride started for Broken Olla's home in Snaketown. After Dawn passed her mother-in-law's test, grinding the wheat to fine perfection and making soft, hot tortillas for breakfast, the village crier shouted the news. "There will be a feast and wedding ceremonial dance in four days — Dawn and Broken Olla are man and wife!"

Dawn was gracious at the feast and received the gifts of her new relatives with smiles. It was both a glad time and a sad time for the lovely young girl. But she would not show her sad feelings to anyone. She was a woman now, a Pima woman in the old tradition. Brave, hard-working, modest, and wise, Dawn would bear many children and live to a ripe old age, a tribute to the teachings of her strict old Pima family.

A First and Final Battle

AT FIRST RED ARROW deeply missed his beautiful older sister whose quiet hard work had made life in the olas kih so comfortable. But soon rumbling rumors of a war trail began to replace Dawn in his thoughts.

"What will the enemy look like? Will I be afraid in battle?" Red Arrow turned these questions over and over in his mind. Finally one night Woodpecker came to him with words that resolved his musings.

"Alge'el (son), the warriors will go on the war trail at dawn. You have learned the art of the kawad well, and the time has come to test your skill. Have your weapons ready before the sun comes up."

"Yes, ni-mahm," replied Red Arrow respectfully, trying to keep the anxiety from his voice. "Will brother Hard Wheat go too?" Red Arrow's whole body was shaking with fear, try though he might to control it.

"Yes, Red Arrow, your brother will go with you," said Woodpecker reassuringly. "And if you find yourself in trouble, your Uncle Turtle will also be there to help." The father smiled in sympathy as he saw his son's nervous reaction. Red Arrow was now stamping his feet, trying to hide his quaking.

"Do not be ashamed, my son," said Woodpecker. "It is natural to have fear. All new warriors shake before a battle. Now go tell Hard Wheat, ready your weapons, and then go to sleep. You must be well rested for the ordeal ahead."

The two excited brothers carefully checked their war clubs and bows and arrows. Red Arrow lovingly touched his little round war shield. "May you protect me well, my friend," he thought. All night long he bravely brandished the little kawad in his dreams.

*   *   *

Before dawn Red Arrow was awakened by his brother, who nudged him and whispered, "Wake up! It is time for the war trail. The warriors just passed by and we must hurry to catch up with them!"

The two boys helped each other paint their faces, blacken their eyes with black mots clay, and tie bunches of feathers to the backs of their heads. They checked to see that they had all their weapons and saw to it that their water gourds were filled. Finally they tied little sacks of Grandmother Red Flowers' nourishing pinole to their belts.

Like two sneaky coyotes the brothers left the olas kih. The Pimas had the tradition of never awakening their loved ones upon leaving for the war trail. It was hard and painful enough for those who remained at home. Who knew what fates might await their dear ones in the battle?

In no time the two swift boys had joined the war party in their trek into the area north of the Salt River, where the wary Apache always roamed. When the sun was directly overhead, they stopped under a shady tree to rest and eat their lunch of whole wheat tortillas. Some also partook of the pinole on their belts.

Red Arrow was shaking, but he gulped down his food. After lunch, his stomach was still growling. "Are you also still hungry, Hard Wheat?" he whispered to his brother.

"Stop complaining, Red Arrow," chided the older boy. "Warriors are tough! They are not supposed to grumble!"

Embarrassed, Red Arrow arose and joined the march toward the hills in the area near what is now Carl Pleasant Dam in the Bradshaw Mountains. On the trail they found a man fast asleep under a tree. He looked like a Pima, but to be sure one brave asked in the Pima tongue, *"Nap si kohsh?* (Are you asleep?)" The man awoke, startled. He understood not a word of the brave's question, but he did know that he had been surrounded by a Pima war party. Without another thought he started to flee, but he was too late to escape the Pima arrows. This was indeed one of the foe.

Red Arrow was all eyes as he stared down at the fallen man. "So this is the enemy," he thought. In reality, the man looked very much like a Pima. As Red Arrow found himself quailing at the idea of killing such a familiar-looking brave, he brought to mind his father's question: "Are you ready to take the place of some old warrior when he retires from battle?" He had been so confident when he answered yes that day — now he must make good his promise and be brave and ready to kill like his Uncle Turtle. To maintain his confidence, Red Arrow kept his eye on Turtle's strong, determined back as the war party trudged over the rugged mountains.

Within a short time the Pimas came upon the enemy war

party, and with whoops and yells a battle began by the side of a hill. Red Arrow found himself caught up in the middle of the fray, too occupied with his own hand-to-hand skirmishes to even notice what was happening to those about him. He felt numb and clammy with fear, but Uncle Turtle's strict training served him well. Although he cut off no enemy scalps as trophies, he defended himself admirably from the onslaughts of Apache braves older and more experienced than himself. His shield and agile dodging saved him from enemy arrows, while his war club lashed out and caused more than one foe to flee with a painful headache.

Once, during a lull in the battle, Red Arrow saw one of his friends trip on a loose rock, fall, and roll down a steep hill. Others saw him too, and they jeered loudly, calling him a coward for running away from the enemy.

The unfortunate young man sat near a bush with tears in his eyes, his head bowed, his heart filled with shame. He knew he would be the butt of the warriors' jokes for a long time. His sad, downcast face made him look as though he had lost his last horse.

Komadk Shon (Flat Base) went over to him and spoke words of comfort. "Don't mind the ridicule. It is all in fun. The braves only want to help you to be always on the alert. We know you will do better next time. The first battle is always the hardest one for a young warrior."

Red Arrow felt sorry for his friend. In his heart he knew it could just as easily have been himself. The thought made him even more alert and intent when another young Apache approached him, shouting war cries and challenges.

When the foe saw that many of their number had

fallen, they ran and disappeared into the surrounding hills. Red Arrow watched them flee, wiping the sweat and dust from his face and breathing a long sigh of relief.

The leader of the Pima war party made motions with raised hands and hollered, "G wo i hihim! Come!" The braves all followed him, shouting the Pima war cry, "Hipah! Hipah! Haia Ohb!" Red Arrow yelled the loudest, filled with pride at the victory. The hills resounded with echoes.

*   *   *

Tired but happy, the Pima warriors trudged homeward. At the first rest stop the leader requested a runner to run home to relate the news of the victory, citing all those braves who had taken hair trophies. Red Arrow whispered to Hard Wheat, "My name will not be called. I did not kill an enemy."

"So what, my brother?" asked Hard Wheat. "I did not kill either, but that is no cause for shame. We are still alive. Be glad of it, Red Arrow!"

When the party reached their beloved Gila, they made a temporary camp away from their homes. As always after a battle, they had to stay isolated for ritual purification. If this rule were not observed, evil spirits would bring sickness and even death. After all, they had been in close bodily contact with the enemy, breathing in their breaths. Some had killed and stood before the face of death.

Daily baths were taken by the warriors, and all whiffed ban wiwga, coyote tobacco, to kill the spirits of evil. Red Arrow found the rest refreshing and welcome, but he was anxious to return to his family and friends, who would hold a feast and a dance to celebrate the victory and home-coming.

At the great festival, Woodpecker spoke to his youngest son with pride in his voice. "You have gained your man-hood, my boy, and killed your first coyote." Red Arrow beamed at the words of praise, especially the last ones, for often his father had discouraged him from joining the warriors in the village council house with the same old expression: "My son, you may not go until you have killed your first coyote." Now things would be different.

Throughout the night Red Arrow danced and feasted and tried not to boast. He no longer regretted not having cut off an enemy hair trophy for his belt. Perhaps that would happen next time.

*　　*　　*

But Red Arrow did not know, as he dreamed of future victories, that there would be no next time. That skirmish with the Apache in the Bradshaw Mountains was to be the last battle the Pima braves would ever fight.

The white man had been pressuring Chief Antonio Azul to lay down his weapons and live peaceably with the Apache. The wise old chief could see that the old way of life was changing and agreed that it was time to stop the earth's rumblings and tremblings in war.

A council was held to resolve many important matters. One of the topics was marriage. An Apache chief declared, "When one of your Pima boys decides to marry one of our Apache girls, he must bring money, horses, and other valuable gifts to her parents."

Chief Azul emphatically shook his head in the negative:

Chief Antonio Azul was my *wihkol* — a distant relative on my mother's side. But in the old days we felt close to all our relations, so mother would take me to visit the great chief. I remember him as a very old wise man, as in this picture, but I have been told that in his youth he was a fiery and handsome example of Pima manhood.

"No! No! It is not right! It would be the same as buying your daughter. The families on both sides must bring gifts to the young couple to help them start their home. We Pimas call this custom *kih shondath* (house foundation)."

In a similar manner Antonio Azul's good judgment helped iron out many other differences in custom between the two tribes. Peace was declared, and the mountains never again rang with the yells of angry warriors.

Although glad for peace, Red Arrow often felt sad when he saw his little kawad gathering dust on the rafters of the olas kih. It had served him well in his first and final battle. How small and useless it looked in times of peace!

Pima Love and Marriage

RED ARROW WAS RESTLESS, for there was nothing exciting to do. No target practice, no shield lessons, no war trails. He had already helped his father harvest the crops and plant more seeds, for it was *shopol eshabig* (short planting season). Now there was only hunting to fill the time, and one could not hunt all day.

When Woodpecker saw Red Arrow lying about bored and unhappy, he made a suggestion: "Son, why don't you go meet the boys at the Casa Blanca store? It is not good to stay home too much."

So Red Arrow saddled his pony and rode to the white man's store. He joined a group of Pima young people who lolled about the meeting place talking and eating sugar cubes, crackers, and cheese.

Before long, a maiden named Haus Molly caught Red Arrow's eye. She had long shiny black hair and stood straight and tall. Red Arrow was shy at first, but soon he gained enough courage to buy her some sugar cubes. The two ate the sweets together, smiling at each other with their eyes. Before long Red Arrow lived only for his daily visits with the maiden at the store.

At home Hard Wheat noticed Red Arrow's behavior. "Red Arrow is in love! He has a *ma'ishpa* (sweetheart)!" he teased.

Red Arrow glanced at him irritably and left the olas kih. His ma'ishpa should not be spoken of in fun.

One day Red Arrow, now fifteen, spoke seriously to his father about marriage. He told him of Molly's beauty and virtue, but his father seemed more interested in her parents. He was satisfied to discover that Molly was the eldest of five daughters of *S-chuk Kamish* (Black Shirt), a great and wise warrior. Woodpecker had seen the deep scars this old fighter bore upon his legs, the evidence of many battles. He remembered that Black Shirt was a distant relative of the great Chief Antonio Azul, one of those honored by the chief in being chosen to go as a scout with the white soldiers when they made peace with the Yumas on the Colorado River.

Black Shirt's wife *Ne'i Kuhkug* (Song Endings) was a hard-working and virtuous woman. There were two boys in the family — *Ha-wokai* and *Lohwie*. Woodpecker recalled that the old warrior also had a second wife. He was popular among the Maricopas and spoke their language fluently. In fact, it was they who had given him the nickname Black Shirt.

"It will be a good family to join with," thought Woodpecker. "You have chosen well, son," he said aloud. "Now you must find a man whose voice is pleasant to be your proxy and plead on your behalf to Molly's parents. After you have found such a flowery speechmaker, you must wait four days before you go with him to ask for the maiden's hand.

Before Christianity was brought to the Pimas, a brave could have as many wives as he could support. For most men this was only one. My Grandfather Black Shirt, however, had a second wife, the woman beside him in this picture. I have heard that his first wife, my Grandmother Song Endings, was the one who stayed home and did all the work.

Red Arrow made his appointment with the speech-maker, and in four days they set out for Molly's olas kih in Sacate. Black Shirt met them at the doorway. When they stated the purpose of their visit, the old warrior asked them inside. Red Arrow sat at the door while the speech-maker settled beside Molly's father.

"This young man, Red Arrow, would like to marry your daughter Molly. He is the son of Woodpecker. He is strong and a good worker. His name is not loud because he stays at home working with his father. Someday he will own cattle."

Black Shirt was pleased to hear the good words. But he told them, "Molly must decide for herself." The Indian maiden remained silent, which meant that she would accept Red Arrow. Had she turned her back and answered no, the suitor and speechmaker would get the hint and return home, and the marriage would not take place.

Red Arrow's heart jumped when he saw that Molly was willing. In the old Pima tradition, he remained at her olas kih for four nights. Then he took his bride home to his father's house in Santa Cruz.

The old ones, Red Flowers and Gray Owl, offered Molly their warmest greetings. Woodpecker proudly pre-sided at a great feast while friends and relatives came to meet the new bride and bring gifts for the young couple. It was a time of great happiness, for a new young woman had become a part of the family.

*   *   *

From the beginning Molly was tested, just as Dawn had been. She too knew that on her first night in her new home she must grind the wheat which had been left near the metate and make the breakfast tortillas to show her industry. A bride who stopped grinding before the job was done was considered lazy and worthless.

Even though she was only sixteen, Molly knew how to care for a household. As was expected of her, she took over the duties of food-gathering, cooking, and caring for Red Arrow and his family. She went about her work with industry, for she knew she must prove herself to her new family.

Red Arrow was proud of his wife and her fine cooking. He loved her succotash made with brown beans, wheat, and soup bone. Her pinole, made from roasted ground wheat, tasted as good and chewy as Dawn's. She knew how to roast beef, venison, antelope, horse meat, fish, and locusts to perfection. She expertly jerked left-over meat in the sun for future meals.

Molly's bean pot was always filled with good-smelling things, even in the summer when her days were often spent gathering wild foods in the desert. In late June and early July, she would join the other women as they took their long *ku'ipad* (saguaro rib poles) out among the giant cacti to harvest the sweet red fruit. After boiling it into a syrup, she stored it away for winter use in little ollas with round clay lids. The tiny black seeds were shaped into balls and stored; nothing was wasted. A portion of Molly's syrup always went into the large community ollas to ferment into wine for the rain-making ceremonies. During this festival, Molly would join the other women on top of the olas kih, where they made fun of the men, who grew silly and clumsy from drinking the fermented fruit.

Photo by Helga Teiwes-French, Arizona State Museum, Tucson

Except for her outfit, this modern Papago woman harvesting saguaro fruit looks much like my mother Molly in the days of old. Later in the season the low cholla cacti in this picture will also bear juicy fruit, but Indians of today no longer eat it. They leave this delicacy for their cattle.

After the saguaro gathering came foraging for the buds of the prickly pear and cholla cacti. After picking the fruit with two sticks used like scissors, she placed it in a rough willow basket made to fit her side. Then she roasted it all night on layers of sagebrush in a pit among the rocks. In the morning, she would carefully pull off the thorns, then dry and store the fruit for the winter months.

When caterpillars were plentiful, Molly would gather them in large quantities, cut off their heads, and squeeze out their insides. Then she boiled them in salted water, and when they were cooked, she salted them again before braiding them into long strands for storage.

Next her saguaro rib poles were brought out again — this time to harvest the bean pods of the mesquite tree. Off and on during the hot month of July Molly would fill her *gioho* (burden basket) with *wihog* (mesquite pods). She would smile as she watched the village youngsters climb the trees and stamp their feet to shake down the pods for their mothers. The mesquite bean pods were an important staple in the Pima diet. Molly would dry them in the sun, then pound them to a powder in a wooden mortar with a long stone pestle. The powder was made into cakes for nourishment during the winter famine.

Sometimes Molly would bring a sharp stone ax and olla instead of her saguaro rib pole. She would scrape the ax at the black gum of the mesquite until she had a sufficient quantity for a beauty treatment. After she had dried the gum for several days, she would pound it to a powder in her wooden mortar. The black powder was then mixed with the sticky black mud from the irrigation ditch. When the mixture was right, she put the mud pack in an earthen

jar and allowed rotting to take place for three or four days.
When all was ready, she would plaster each strand of her
long black hair with the mud pack. Then she tied a cloth
tightly about her head to prevent dripping. The next day
the pack would be dry but heavy. Molly would be relieved
when breakfast was over and she could go to the river to
wash off the mud. But she always felt the torture was
worthwhile when she saw how the mud pack had made
her long hair more beautiful, black, and lustrous. Even
Red Arrow and the other braves often underwent this
treatment, for all Pimas are very proud of their hair and
keep it very clean.

If Red Arrow's new wife wasn't out in the desert, she
might be found in the fields with her husband. In the late
summer, when the Indian corn was ripe, she would gather
a large pile of mesquite wood and place two or three dozen
ears of green corn among the twigs. When a match struck
the bottom of the wood pile, the corn was roasted. The
process was repeated until the desired amount was prepared. When it was cool, Molly husked the corn and spread
it in the sun on top of the brush ramada to dry. The
parched corn, called *ga'iwesa,* was ground on a metate
with a mano, or rolling stone. Red Arrow especially liked
it when it was fried and seasoned with red chile.

When the muskmelons and squash were ripe, Molly
again went to the fields to help cut them into strips, then
hang them to dry in the sun. She added the strips to her
winter stores, to eat with or without lard when fresh vegetables were not available.

Because she was so industrious, Molly's huge storage
baskets were filled by the time winter came. Besides wheat,

saguaro syrup, cholla fruit, caterpillars, mesquite cakes, parched corn, melon strips, and squash, they contained dried salt bush leaves to flavor winter foods in the cooking pot. Next to the great storage baskets, animal skin bags held the jerky Molly had put up for winter meals. There was honey for sweetening and salt for seasoning. From the ceiling hung bunches of willow twigs, cattails, and devil's claws for weaving baskets on winter days.

*   *   *

But as she surveyed her full store house, Molly felt grieved. Crop failure had struck their relatives, the Salt River inhabitants, and winter would surely be a time of famine for them. She was relieved when Red Arrow told her that the people of the Santa Cruz Village had decided to give a Name-Calling Dance for their less-fortunate friends.

The men of the village held a council and appointed a man of great knowledge and wisdom to go to Salt River to invite the people to the festival and receive the names of all the families there. This information had to be stored in his memory before he ran back to Santa Cruz to give the names – seventy in all – to the songmaker.

A runner went about the homes, telling the people to bring in beans, corn, wheat, melons, and squash – anything that was edible. Those families fortunate enough to have extra stores of mesquite cakes, saguaro syrup, or cholla fruit added these delicacies for good measure.

Red Arrow helped the men put the heavy bundles of food into baskets and homemade bags of coarsely woven cotton. They were careful to see that all the people would receive the same amount. As they worked, the group of singers was busy learning the Name-Calling songs.

When the big day arrived, people came from all directions. A great feast was prepared, and all ate their fill before the dance began. The singers sat on a well-swept place with their beautifully designed baskets turned upside down. At first they gently rubbed the baskets with their notched sticks to make a soft sound. Then the mixed voices of men and women began. When the notched sticks became louder, it was a sign for the festival singers to begin to sing.

Huai Nohnhowi (Deer Arms) was the first name called in the song. He chose his wife to be his partner in the round dance. This process went on for a long, long time until all the names were called and everyone from Salt River was dancing.

When the dance was over, a speech was made by the leader of the festival. The Salt River people were asked to find the farm products that had been placed here and there near the dance grounds for each family to take home for their winter use. It wouldn't be right not to return the speech, so a Salt River man noted for speechmaking went to the front of the throng of people and gave his talk. He told the Santa Cruz villagers how happy they had made his people of the Salt River. The winter famine could not touch them because of the gifts. Molly and Red Arrow were filled with joy because they had had enough to help their relatives.

Before the guests left for home, they went among the people expressing their kinship — uncle, cousin, great-grandmother, and many other relationships. Each expression was repeated four times in the old tradition, and the Santa Cruz people responded in kind. Aunt *Melhog Heosig* (Ocotillo) came up to Molly and took her hand: "My niece, my niece, my niece, my niece," she said. Molly smiled and returned, "My aunt, my aunt, my aunt, my aunt." It was a good way to show their love for one another.

*   *   *

After the echoes of the Name-Calling Dance had died away, the winter passed quickly for Haus Molly and Red Arrow. In addition to Molly's stores of dried foods, there was often fresh meat from Red Arrow's hunting trips. Fish was another treat. Red Arrow would catch them with a *wuliwga* — a bundle of willow branches — which he dragged in the water. The fish would flee to a corner near the bank where he and his friends could catch them with their bare hands.

When she finally heard the roadrunner, Molly knew that spring was almost with them. Relieved and happy that the rains would soon bring fresh wild foods, she at last dug into her store of nourishing mesquite cakes and served them to the family. After the rains, the danger of starvation was past. The desert sprouted with delicious fresh salt bush leaves, which Molly gathered and boiled like spinach or served fresh like salad. Berries began to form, and the cacti bloomed with beautiful flowers which would become sweet fruit. Red Arrow and Woodpecker went out to make the fields ready for seed. Spring was a glad time of year; they had made it through another winter.

The Responsibilities of Manhood

AFTER HE WAS MARRIED, Red Arrow often wondered how he could have thought that village life was boring. Now his problem was finding enough hours in the day to care for his fields and livestock and still pursue some of the leisure activities adult male Pimas enjoyed.

Woodpecker, like many elderly men, was still spry enough to help with the farming, but the fact remained that he was getting old. Now he spent more time in the council house, smoking, listening to stories, and telling some himself.

In the spring, when cultivating and planting must be done, Woodpecker would join the other old men who went out to gather *a'ut* (mescal). This delicacy, loved by many Southwestern Indians, including the Apaches, grew in the mountains around the village. The old men would make a holiday of it, camping out for three or four days. They would cut the tender lower stem and leaves of each huge succulent plant just as it was beginning to sprout. This inner portion, which resembled an artichoke, was chopped and baked in a pit among hot rocks all night and a part of the next day. When it was roasted and cooled, the men divided the delicious sweet among themselves to

Threshing was always a kind of holiday, even though it was hard, hot work. Here was our chance to exchange news and gossip with our friends the Papagos, who came to help us with the chore. Often romances developed under the summer moon, and so the Pimas have many relatives among the Desert People.

take home to their families. The sap was sometimes fermented, making a beverage the old ones claimed had a "kick like a mule."

Red Arrow loved the mescal Woodpecker brought back, but he missed him in the fields for those four days. The young man realized that the time had come to take on the responsibilities of manhood. This meant being the one in charge of making sure the family would have plenty to eat.

Early in the morning Red Arrow would go out to the family fields to cultivate with a heavy mesquite-wood plow. Fertilizer was never necessary, for when melting mountain snows and spring rains filled the Gila, it overflowed its banks, spreading black loam over the Pima farms. Each person in the family helped to plant the seeds in the rich soil with a pointed mesquite stick called a *gihk*. After the hole was dug with the gihk, the bare heels pushed in dirt to cover the seed.

Besides wheat, beans, corn, cotton, muskmelons, and squash, Red Arrow grew a patch of juicy watermelons. These were a favorite fruit of the Pimas, and when the melons were ripe there were always visitors at Red Arrow's olas kih. Sometimes the men fermented the juice into a mildly alcoholic drink.

Late summer and fall meant harvest time. Red Arrow and his family harvested most of the crops themselves, but they frequently had help with the wheat. Often the Papagos came from the south to aid with this chore.

Harvesting in those days was very primitive. The wheat was cut with a sickle, put in little piles, then tied into bundles and put on a wagon. The wagon would take it to a cleared threshing place nearby. The Pimas still threshed in the manner taught them by Father Kino, with horses trampling the grain from the chaff as they walked about a pole. Then the grain was separated by being thrown up in the breeze.

The Papago women usually did this last job. They too were marvelous basket weavers, but the devil's claws which the Pimas used to form their beautiful black designs did not grow in the desert country. So after they had finished the dusty chore of threshing, the women would go along the irrigated fields and gather the devil's claws into little piles. When they departed for Papago land, they carried the bundles with them to use in their weaving.

While the Papagos were helping with the wheat, Red Arrow would be going about his regular daily chores, tending the family cattle and horses and driving them to the river to drink. When the grass was scarce, he would feed them hay. In between these jobs, he had to fit in hunting and fishing.

*   *   *

But being a man brought pleasures as well as responsibilities. Now Red Arrow could sit with the men in the village council house, smoking coyote tobacco and listening to news of the villages and stories of war. He never spoke but listened as the experienced elders told their tales.

Red Arrow especially liked the stories told by *Jusigol* (Lizard). Once this old warrior told a strange tale about the Apaches:

"We were anxious to repay the Mexicans for the dirty deal they put over on us. You know how they would sell their cattle to us. When the cattle would go back to them, they would bring the beasts back and resell them to us again. We soon caught on to their tricks.

"We headed toward Tucson full of anger in our hearts. When we were near Picacho Peak, one of the braves discovered moccasin tracks in the sand. It was decided that we must return home, since there were too few of us to fight with the Apaches.

"We sang all night to keep up our spirits. Just as we expected, before dawn we were returning Apache arrows that fell heavily around us like a rainstorm. In dodging our arrows, one of the Apaches ran smack into a giant saguaro cactus. He screamed in pain and ran back toward his own country, the rest of his band following.

"We figured the band thought that evil spirits had hurt the warrior, and we were relieved to see them leave. We couldn't guess what had caused the cries of pain, since it was too dark to see the tall cactus. But when the dawn came, we could see the fresh footprints around it.

"I don't mind telling how scared we were because the odds were so against us," ended Lizard. "We lost one of our young men in the skirmish."

Another old fighter told a story about a stubborn mule:

"The Apache marauders came to one of the *Tohono O'othham* (Desert People; Papago) villages in the night and quietly left without hurting the villagers. Early in the morning, their moccasin tracks were discovered. They had stolen three ponies and one mule. While the Papagos were standing around feeling sorry for their loss, they saw a man riding a mule toward the village.

"As the rider came near, the Indians saw him pulling at the mule's bridle to turn him around, but without luck. The stubborn mule came into camp with the Apache rider still on his back. The Papago men surrounded him, and another foe was wiped out."

One of Red Arrow's favorite smoke house tales concerned the brave deed of one of his uncles, *Bihimsani* (Binder), nicknamed *Soam I'ipudaj* (Yellow Dresses). Lizard often told the story:

"Near where the Verde and the Salt rivers flow together stands the *Sawik* (Red Mountain). Its origins are lost in time, but to the Pimas it became Sawik because of the redness of its earth and its red glow at sunset.

"In those early days, no Pima would dare to venture alone near the Sawik. Whenever a band of Pima warriors passed near the Red Mountain, Apaches were waiting to scalp them. Many a bloody skirmish took place near its base; a lone Pima had little chance of making it by the mountain.

"Early one morning some young Pima boys were at Maricopa Wells. They were adventuresome and hardy braves, who liked to talk in Spanish to the soldiers stationed there. Sometimes the soldiers would throw away their old clothing, which the half-naked Pimas would appropriate for their own use.

"One morning a soldier walked up to the braves, who were playing a game of *gins*. He asked for a volunteer to deliver an important message to Fort McDowell, called

O'otkam Wa'akih (Sandy Mound) by the Pimas. Ten dollars would be the payment for the one who made the journey.

"The Indian lads were silent. They knew it was dangerous Apache country near the Sawik and that they would have to pass through it in order to reach the fort. They shrugged their shoulders and refused to volunteer, even for the money.

"At last Yellow Dresses stepped forward. 'I will go,' he said. All the dark eyes looked at the volunteer. 'Are you not afraid of the Ohb?'

"Yellow Dresses was given a folded paper with black marks on it. He was instructed to wave a white cloth upon his arrival to let the soldiers know he was bearing a message.

"The Pima brave galloped away to the northeast. When he crossed the Salt River just a short distance from the lookout point of the Red Mountain, he knew he was in the land of the Apaches. His hair felt as though it were standing up. He urged the mule to hurry, but no incident occurred until he was almost at the fort.

"The soldiers saw the approaching Indian brave and started to shoot at him. Then Yellow Dresses took out the white cloth and waved. As suddenly as it had started, the shooting stopped. The soldiers came out on foot and surrounded their surprised visitor.

"Yellow Dresses could not understand what they were saying, so the white soldiers used sign language. They took his mule and put it in the corral to be fed and watered. Yellow Dresses was led inside, and motions were made for him to sit and eat. After feeding him, the soldiers gave him a cot to sleep on that night. 'So this is how it feels to sleep in a soft bed!' he thought.

"In the Indian custom, Yellow Dresses awoke before the sun was up and started on his homeward journey. He had only gone a short way when he heard the hooves of the soldiers' horses. Looking back, he wondered, 'Now what have I done?' As the soldiers caught up with him, fear rose once again inside him; but they only motioned him to go back to the fort for breakfast. Then they followed him to protect him until he had crossed the Salt River below Red Mountain.

"Here they stopped and waved at him: 'Adios! adios!' It was all so strange to the Pima brave. He could not understand why the soldiers should do all this for him. 'Such kind and generous gringos!' he thought.

"The ten dollars Yellow Dresses received in payment for his trip was a large sum in those days. And for the rest of his life, the sight of Red Mountain served as a silent reminder of his courage."

Some of the council house talk consisted of short anecdotes, and Red Arrow learned from these also. He remembered two in particular:

Once before a battle, a Yuma chief said to a Maricopa warrior, "I am ready to have you strike me first if you can."

"It is for me to let you try your club on me. You wanted to kill me, and you have traveled far to satisfy your heart," answered the Maricopa.

Once the white soldiers met the Pima warriors in the

road, carrying soldier weapons. Immediately the Indians were accused of stealing. The Pimas made sign language for the whites to follow them. When they found some of their white soldiers and Apaches lying dead in the desert, then and only then did they believe the Pima warriors, who had always aided them in the Apache wars.

Chukud Nahk (Owl Ear) made this unforgettable remark to his warriors: "That is why I do not think the white man is good enough to trust us."

Some of the historical events recounted in the smoke house were also recorded by the village calendar stick keeper. Every Pima village had one of these men to keep track of important occurrences. Owl Ear was the calendar stick keeper for the Salt River Reservation, while *Ko'owi Mo'okam* (Rattlesnake Head) served Gila Crossing and Juan Thomas served Blackwater.

The calendar stick was a dry saguaro cactus rib two inches wide and four feet long. Interesting marks, which reminded the calendar stick keeper of important happenings, were carved upon its surface. When the analyst was asked about an event, he would slowly run his fingers over the carved stick, and with a faraway look he would tell the record of a certain year.

Red Arrow loved to listen to the calendar stick keeper. The events related by him and by the old men in the smoke house taught him about past triumphs and mistakes and gave him lessons which he could apply to his own life.

*   *   *

But listening to tales was not Red Arrow's only leisure activity. Like most Pima males, he liked to gamble, losing many a good horse and blanket during games of *gins* and *woptha*. When he wanted more active fun he could always find a friend to practice running with him. His strong, healthy body and keen mind gave him the advantage, and he not only frequently won the one-mile race, but was a formidable runner in the great race, which covered more than twenty-five miles.

Red Arrow's prowess at running also served him well in his favorite sport of *wuichutha,* or kickball. This game was played with a small, smoothly whittled wooden ball covered with creosote gum. The ball was thrown on the ground in the road, and the player ran and kicked the ball straight ahead with his bare feet, with the right big toe usually going into action. If he was skillful, the ball would stay on the road; otherwise it would roll into the desert brush, and the player had to chase after it. He couldn't pick it up with his hands; he had to kick it back to the road. Many a sore toe resulted from this sport! The winner was the one who reached a designated finish line first. Many bets were placed on the contestants, and spirits ran high during a game.

Red Arrow practiced wuichutha whenever he could. When he drove his livestock down to the Gila, the little ball could always be seen rolling along in front of him. It was not long before the men in charge of setting up matches noticed Red Arrow's developing skill and asked him to participate in the competition with other villages. Soon he had a reputation for excellence.

Once he was pitted against a young man of Wah'akih. The two stood on the line until they heard the count: *hemako* (one), *gohk* (two), *waik* (three)! *Thohwa'i!*

Owl Ear, the Salt River calendar stick keeper, had a gift for telling stories as well as a good memory. Some of the events recorded on his stick also appear in history books, although the Pimas often attached significance to happenings the white man thought unimportant. They just had different ways of seeing things.

The players threw their balls into the road and began to run and kick them. Soon Red Arrow was ahead. He dared not look back, for he had to keep his eyes always on the little round weech-da ball to see where it landed after each kick. He tried not to be distracted by the excited spectators, who were laughing and yelling encouragement to their favorite players. Some members of the crowd ran or rode their ponies along the side of the road, cheering the players on. *"Si g mehl! si g mehl!* (Run! run!)" they hollered. A few of the more enthusiastic spectators shouted challenging and mocking remarks at the supporters of the opponent. Sometimes these words came to blows, adding to the excitement.

In the midst of the commotion, Red Arrow heard his opponent cry, *"Si ni gewtan!* (Whip me!)" A horse whip fell on the shoulders of the player from Wah'akih. What sort of strange thing was this? Just then Red Arrow heard one of the Wah'akih spectators ask the same question, "Why whip him?"

"Because he asked me before the starting point to whip him if he should lag behind, spurring him on to victory," replied the man with the horse whip.

But the strange encouragement was to no avail. "Red Arrow has already reached the end of the trail!" shouted *S-kohmagi* (Gray). "Red Arrow is the winner!"

Red Arrow was tired, thirsty, and covered with dust. His eyelashes and long hair were colored like a *s-kohmagi o'othham* (gray Indian). He had to catch his breath and take a long drink of water before he joined the men to settle the results of the betting. That day Red Arrow won money, yards of calico for Molly, and a fine new horse.

As he left the game area, loaded down with bright yard goods, a friend stopped him. "I'm glad you won, *Al O'obab*," he said, calling Red Arrow by his nickname, Maricopa. "I bet my best pony on you!"

A New Way of Life

SUPPORTING A FAMILY, smoking in the council house, and winning in sports events were important parts of Pima manhood. But Red Arrow never felt entirely grown up until the day that Molly presented him with their first child, a daughter named Juana. He would never forget the joy he felt as he raised the little girl to the Sun God. But neither would he forget his sorrow when their next child, a little boy, died.

Red Arrow and Molly had eleven children in all. Of these, only five lived to adulthood. Whooping cough, measles, and other white man's sicknesses took some of them. And Molly became convinced that a lack of knowledge of rules of hygiene and disease prevention was responsible for some of the deaths.

She would later tell her youngest daughter: "I see you dress your children up and cover them with warm blankets. We never had such things in our time: just a little cotton rag woven by the old men. And we weren't educated to know that it was wrong to take the babies out when they had a cold, so when we did they caught pneumonia and died. I lost so many of my babies because of things I did not know about."

But life was changing for Red Arrow and Haus Molly. Soon they would learn many strange new things.

*   *   *

In 1870 a kind and gentle man named Charles H. Cook arrived to live among the Pimas. This *mil-gahn* (white man) was different from anyone the River People had ever known. He told them of the Gospel message, but he was different from the Spanish missionary priests of long ago. He called himself a Presbyterian.

Within two years of his arrival, Dr. Cook had acquired the Pima language and an understanding of the culture. He began to teach the children by giving them crackers and cube sugar. In a tiny adobe building near Sacaton, he tried to teach them English and the three R's. Wherever he went he was kind and helpful and preached the Gospel. On Sundays he held services for a handful of Indians.

At first the Pimas were slow to accept Dr. Cook's teachings. They had experienced many broken treaties, and unscrupulous traders and agents had made them even more suspicious of the white man. The medicine men were especially opposed to the Gospel message, for they felt it would destroy the old beliefs. Probably they also feared losing their customers, for Dr. Cook talked of a new kind of medicine.

But despite all obstacles, the determined missionary persevered in his efforts. He believed in the Pimas and felt that to educate the Indian, his soul must be touched.

Dr. Cook's heavy load was made lighter when a young German lady with whom he corresponded agreed to come to Sacaton to start life with him. Anna Cook was a real helpmate, working side by side with her husband. Their marriage was blessed with eight wonderful children.

*   *   *

It was twelve years before the Cooks reaped their first converts. Chief Antonio Azul was among them. Many times during those hard early days, the great chief had helped Dr. Cook make the people see the importance of education in the white man's way. Once the missionary had overheard a group of advisers urging the chief to go to war with the white intruders. "No!" the chief had answered. "It is wrong to fight! We can learn many lessons from the mil-gahn."

After that first group of Pimas was baptized, Christianity spread like wildfire among the Pimas. Within five years the converts had helped build a little adobe church, where they could sing hymns and worship every Sunday.

Dr. Cook's joy was great as he preached the Word to his enthusiastic congregation. The Indians loved to help in the service. Those who spoke English interpreted the words of the Bible and hymns. Soon all the Pima Christians had learned some of the songs, which were sung with great gusto.

One little old man named Joseph Sankey was so enthusiastic about the hymns that he interested a group of Indians of Salt River, who then traveled in wagons to Gila Crossing to teach others the translated songs. The devout Sankey led the group. He once was heard to say, "I looked back and saw the wagonload of Indians following. It made me think of Moses leading his people in the wilderness. I felt that I was Moses."

It was mostly the women folk who would gather with this wandering choir and sing all day. Their husbands would be out working in the fields, unaware of Joseph Sankey's arrival. When work was over, however, they found out soon enough, for their wives were gone, and the bean pots were empty. They were upset, of course, but later they too joined the singers.

The village people met in the homes in the evenings to sing until the sun peeped over the eastern mountains. My how those early Christians loved to sing and pray! Enthusiasm for learning lifted their spirits and changed their old way of life. Many were baptized.

In the midst of such success, Dr. Cook had to face sorrow when his seven-year-old boy suddenly passed away. He was soon followed by his courageous mother, who caught cold from the rain which leaked through the roof of their rough home. Weakened by years of hard living, Mrs. Cook died on December 18, 1889.

Dr. Cook remained faithful to his mission, despite the loss of his dear ones. The seed of Christianity he planted germinated and grew steadily on the banks of the Gila. More and more Pimas were being baptized by Cook.

*   *   *

But there was one Pima who would have no part of the new ways. Red Arrow saw no reason to give up the old Pima gods and beliefs. Shortly after his marriage he had moved his family from Santa Cruz Village to a remote little settlement located under a tall, rocky ridge in the Estrella Mountains. As he busily plowed and planted, he often thought disdainfully of the converts who wasted their time singing hymns in church.

If a man was strong and healthy, Red Arrow reasoned, he should have no need for a god of comfort, such as the one of which the Christians spoke. Life was hard, but it was full of good things too. True, he had lost many children, and Gray Owl, Red Flowers, and Woodpecker had gone to join the babies in Si'al Wui. But Haus Molly was alive and healthy, and his son *Waikka S-ehbith* (Afraid of the Ditch) and two married daughters, Molly and Juana, would soon give him grandchildren. In his own olas kih, little *Gaht* (Bow) and *Chehia* (Maiden) were hardy toddlers. With good health and a fine family, who needed a god of salvation and comfort?

In due time Red Arrow was called *Pi Wohochuththam* (Unbeliever). Whenever the villagers invited him to go with them to hear Dr. Cook, he would reply, "Bah! I do not believe the pale face. The earth still gives us roots, berries, and green leaves to eat and herbs to cure our ills. We have the fruit of the tall cactus that we make into good wine to satisfy our thirst. The white man is not to be trusted — he has broken many treaties. No, I will never believe!"

Every Friday, when the small band of converts left the little village, they were mocked and taunted by Red Arrow. "Aw! Your brown skin will never change. Do you not know the white man is here to take our land?"

The devout Christians would only smile patiently. They had a long walk ahead of them before their overnight rest at Casa Blanca. Then they had many more miles of sagebrush to cover before they reached the little adobe church at Sacaton.

One morning, as Red Arrow left his house to mock the Christians, he had a surprise. The men had shorn their long hair, and they wore fine new hats. "Ha! ha!" laughed the Unbeliever. *"Ahi kus hebai?* (Now what?) So you allowed the pale face to cut off your long hair! You look funny! Your heads look like my little round wuichutha balls!" Red Arrow laughed again and gave the Pima war yell, "Hipah, hipah!" The hills resounded and echoed.

Wheela, the first Pima convert, only smiled and tipped his new hat. The rest of the men did likewise and looked with compassion at their tormentor.

But Red Arrow could not deny the force of Christianity much longer. By now some of the local preachers had realized their responsibility to Dr. Cook, and new little adobe churches were beginning to spring up all along the Gila. When a church was finally erected across the river from Red Arrow's remote little farm, gentle Haus Molly decided to join the Christians in their Sunday worship. She left after her husband had gone out to the hills at dawn to hunt antelope and deer. When Red Arrow returned, tired and hungry, he found the olas kih empty and the bean pot cold. One needs little imagination to picture the family spat which occurred when Haus Molly finally crawled through the low doorway!

But despite Red Arrow's opposition, the next Sunday Molly again attended church. Rather than stay home alone, Red Arrow went to visit his good friend José, who lived on a little knoll near the church.

"*Ni-nawoj* (my friend), you are here just in time to go to church with me!" said José with warmth. Out of curiosity, Red Arrow decided to go with his pal. "I want to find out why these meetings are attracting so many of my relatives," he told José as they walked.

In the churchyard Red Arrow met his cousin White Soatikee. "*Ni-oh!itha* (my cousin)," repeated White Soatikee four times, in the old Pima tradition. Red Arrow returned the kinship expression four times. "Come with me, Red Arrow," said White Soatikee. "I have a special place."

Red Arrow followed, thinking, "A poor old man like this cousin of mine probably has a seat in the rear of the church." How surprised was the Unbeliever when White Soatikee led him down the aisle to the first bench, right under the preacher's nose! As he sat down, Red Arrow's knees trembled. He heard someone whisper, "Look — there is the Unbeliever!"

Soon Dr. Cook's assistant, Dr. Wynekoop, entered and stood behind a tall box, while Howard Sanderson, the interpreter, stood beside him. The preacher read from a

book that was on the box, and the interpreter spoke in
Pima. Every word stirred the Unbeliever. They seemed
like arrows hitting his heart.

From that day on, every Sunday Red Arrow took his
wife and two small children to the services. In a short time
he decided to join the church, and he asked Molly to cut
off the long matted hair which fell to his waist. It was a
big day when the Unbeliever and his entire family were
baptized by Dr. Wynekoop! Red Arrow was given the
name Josiah Moore; his wife was called Rose. His children also received new names: Jessie, José Newton, Lillie,
William, and Anna.

*   *   *

Red Arrow seldom did anything halfway, and being a
Christian was no exception. With the same intense spirit
with which he had opposed the new ways, he became one
of Dr. Cook's most zealous converts. In a year's time,
Josiah, as he now was called, became an elder. In order
to be closer to the church, he moved his family to Gila
Crossing on the north side of the river. He often gave
cattle to church benefits, and his wife Rose would sew and
make great clay ollas to sell for a dollar.

The new convert also frequently led inspirational sings
in the village homes. Seated on the dirt floor, the Christians
would lift their voices in their native language for the glory
of their new-found faith. In their enthusiasm, many times
the Indians made these meetings sound like competitions
in singing.

Once Josiah turned to an old man and asked, "John, do you have a song you wish to hear?"

"Yes," he replied, "Sing 'Red-Cheeked Baby'."

Josiah smiled, for he realized that this was John's affectionate title for a hymn called "Beautiful Beckoning Hands."

Besides accepting the Gospel message, Josiah became open to many other ways of the white man after he joined the church. The missionaries gave him seeds for grapes, peaches, apricots, and peanuts, and showed him how to grow them. He learned to use new tools for farming, and he received a wagon from the Indian agent when he cut his long hair.

Instead of the breech cloth he had worn all his life, Josiah now wore the white man's clothing. Molly wore ankle-length dresses with long sleeves. Always generous, she made dresses by hand for new women converts.

The old tribal ceremonial dances and the festivals at the little Catholic mission called Saint John's were off limits for good Presbyterians. The missionaries decreed that anyone who attended such events, worked on Sundays, or otherwise sinned would be suspended from the church for a month, unless he confessed in front of the congregation. One old man who habitually sold his watermelons at Saint John's was always confessing. But not Josiah Moore. He now shunned the old beliefs and pastimes, for he had found a better way.

More than anything, Josiah now wanted his children to grow up educated in the white man's manner. He vowed that his youngest children would have the chance to go to school. How sad he felt when he thought of the way he had discouraged his beloved daughter Juana when she had attended the Phoenix Indian School.

*   *   *

Juana, now called Jessie, was Josiah's pride and joy. She was gentle, intelligent, and strikingly beautiful. Everyone said she looked just like her father.

After her marriage, Jessie had gone to live with her husband in Santa Cruz. Josiah had missed her greatly and always looked forward to her visits. She would arrive at the olas kih and ask little Annie, "Where is my mahm?"

"He is not your mahm. He's *my* mahm!" the little girl would reply hotly.

Juana then would laugh musically and tease Annie in her soft, lovely voice: "I believe little sister is jealous!"

One day shortly after the family's baptism, Jessie's husband came to the olas kih on horseback. He spoke to Josiah in low tones, then left again. Immediately Josiah hitched the team to the wagon and started for Santa Cruz with his wife and grown son, Newton.

In the evening they returned with Jessie on a bed of wheat straw in the back of the wagon. The men lifted her and tenderly placed her under the shady arbor.

Dr. Clarence Ellis, missionary and medical doctor, was summoned. He said it was a contagious illness and that the patient should be isolated. Her body was covered with black spots. The Pimas never knew what the disease was called, but in a short time it took Jessie's life.

Although the doctor said that no one should attend the graveside funeral rites, the Indians would not obey but came to comfort the family. Never had they seen Josiah so bereaved. Juana, so newly called Jessie, had been his dearly beloved firstborn.

After his friends left, Josiah sat outside, watching the sunset's colors on the beautiful Estrella Mountains. He wondered how he could have believed that he had no need for the God of Comfort. His terrible loss became easier for him as he repeated the Lord's Prayer in his native language:

Jiosh t-ohg, An ap kihthag t-thahm kahchim ch ed.
Kuch ab si has m-elith ch si haʼichuchuth g m-chehgig.
Ab ach m-tahni mapt wo i geʼethaj g e-kownaltalig ia
       jewed thahm
    mat g m-tatchui am hab wo e junihith
    hab masma mo an hab e wua m-kihthag ed.
Ab g i s-t-hoʼigeʼith k ab wo t-mahkath g haʼichu hugi
       wehs tashkaj.
Gm att hu pi chegito g ha-chuʼichig
      hegam mat hedai pi ap has chuʼi ab t-wui
      ch ab m-tahni mapt hab wa ep wo pi chegito g pi ap
      t-chuʼichig.
Am g i t-nuhkuth ab amjed g pi apʼekam mat pi wo
      t-gewito.
Ahpi ap wud kownal wehs haʼichu thahm ch wehs
      s-gewkthag.
Kutt heg hekaj ab wo si m-ihmath chum hekith.
                    Amen

Education in Two Worlds

LITTLE CHEHIA LOOKED UP at the sun for the twentieth time that afternoon. How slowly it moved across the blue desert sky! Surely it would be forever before brother Willie came home from the Gila Crossing Day School. "No fun without Willie!" the five-year-old remarked, kicking a stone in frustration.

To Chehia it didn't seem fair that Pima children now spent their days in the one-room adobe school houses on the reservation. Her older brothers and sisters had been able to play outdoors all day long! But now everything was different. Ever since the Pimas had started going to church, the mothers and fathers wanted their youngsters to be educated in the white man's way.

For a long time Pima youths who had wanted an education had had no choice but the BIA boarding school in Phoenix or similar schools far away in Grand Junction, Colorado, and Albuquerque, New Mexico. Many people had been opposed to these institutions. Now all sorts of new Indian schools were springing up: little one-room reservation schools like the one Willie attended, the C. H. Cook Christian Training School in Phoenix, and the In-

dian Mission School in Tucson. As soon as they were six
years old, all of Chehia's playmates went to school. Willie
had been attending for two years now. "Bah!" thought
Chehia, "I'm sure I will never be six!"

Just as she was about to look up at the sun once more,
the little girl heard a familiar whistle. "Come on *Hanadka!*
(Fat Belly!)" she called to her dog, and the two took off
at a run to meet brother Willie.

As soon as Willie had changed his clothes, he and
Chehia ran down to the flowing Gila to catch fish. On the
riverbank they looked for *waklu* (driftwood) that was
shaped like long cigars. How unashamedly they smoked
the porous wood! The *chiwi chuhch* (killdeer) lightly
skipped along the shore, and the two happy children imi-
tated it, skipping joyfully on the wet sand.

Sometimes after school Willie would shoot a cottontail, quail, or doves with his bow and arrow. Then it was
always, "Chehia, carry my kill," or "Be quiet, you'll scare
the cottontails."

When it was windy, Willie would make a homemade
wishag (hawk), or kite. How Chehia would squeal as she
watched it flying in the sky, just like the hawks themselves!

One day Willie came home with an exciting announcement. "Ni-tha!al, the teacher wants me to take little sister
Chehia to school with me next week. Christmas will be
here. Santa Claus will come to give us candy."

Chehia was all ears. "She may go," said mother, "but
you must take good care of her. She will feel strange."
Willie's little sister was the happiest child in the whole
village.

Before the big day came, mother took Chehia to the

D. B. Linderman Collection, Arizona State Museum, Tucson

The Gila Crossing Day School stood all by itself on a little rise, near the old-time graveyard in the foreground of this picture. Yet isolated though it was, this schoolhouse provided the only source of the white man's learning for children like Willie and me. To us it represented a whole different world.

running brook and washed her hair. She brushed it over and over with a homemade brush of Sacaton grass to make it shine. Oh, how grown up Chehia felt!

"Mother, don't fill my lunch pail; teacher said school will be dismissed at noon today," said Willie next morning. At last they were on their way!

The mile walk seemed very long to the excited little girl. Finally they passed a graveyard, and Chehia could see the one-room school house on the knoll. Children were playing in the schoolyard. One smart aleck asked, "Hey, Willie, who is the girl? Is she your *oksga* (wife)?" Willie pretended not to have heard. The bell was ringing, and the children ran pellmell into the schoolroom.

Soon every seat was taken. Willie shared his desk with Chehia. "Do you see the chimney?" he asked her. "Santa Claus is going to come down through that chimney."

"What's a chinme?" she asked.

"Aw, don't be so dumb," whispered Willie, pointing to the corner of the room. The little girl caught on and asked, "How can anyone come through that chinme?"

"Don't talk so loud. Don't ask questions. Chehia, you sure need to go to school!" whispered Willie.

But Chehia was too excited to heed Willie's warning. She nudged him with an elbow and asked, "Willie, what is that round thing on the wall? It's making sounds." Willie did not answer her. The little girl thought of her mother and wished that she had stayed at home — mother always answered her questions.

"Willie, what is that pretty cloth with many colors?"

"Chehia, be quiet! You really need to go to school,"

whispered Willie. Then he saw the tears in her eyes and said, "It is called a flag. Now don't be a crybaby. Look at what is happening."

Some older boys and girls were lining up in front of the room. They sang a song, and all of sudden Santa Claus was dancing around. He was a fat man with a bag on his back. Willie's sister wondered, "Did Santha Klaus really come down that chinme?" She did not dare to ask Willie because he might be cross and talk strong again.

In Pima, the teacher explained the meaning of Christmas. His wife placed fruit and candy on all the desks. Chehia picked up a red fruit and asked Willie what it was called.

"Little sister, that is an apple."

"Uh! It is called abble!" She wondered what kind of a tree would bear such pretty fruit! She lifted it up by the stem, and her childlike brain could not imagine such an amazing tree.

After everyone had eaten his candy and fruit, the teacher stood up in front of the class. "No more school until after the Christmas dinner at the Presbyterian church," he said. Then he looked sad and told the children, "I am sorry to have to tell you that after this January I will no longer be your teacher. My school will be at Sacaton. I hope you will be good for your new teacher. School is dismissed. Merry Christmas!"

Mother was weaving a pretty basket when Willie and his sister arrived home. Chehia excitedly told her all about the school and Santha Klaus, the fat little old man with the white hair all around his face.

"You will see him again, Chehia," mother told her. "At the dinner at the church he will bring you a present."

*   *   *

By now readers may be guessing that I was Chehia, or Annie, daughter of Haus Molly and Red Arrow, later called Rose and Josiah Moore. It was 1903, but I still can remember that first church Christmas celebration mother had talked about.

Long tables were laden with food; the Indians gathered around them to eat their fill of steaming beef stew, bread, and a dessert of canned pears, peaches, and apricots. Women hovered about to dish out the food. My mother Rose was one of the cooks. She liked her task as cook, and father always praised her dinners.

John Thomas, one of the first Pima converts, had the job of keeping the dogs from snatching food from the little children. He used a cane to chase the hungry animals away. Sometimes he would tease us by pointing his cane and exclaiming, *"Ge ban! ge ban!* (The coyote! the coyote!)"* We little ones would all run away in fear.

In those times it was difficult to get to Phoenix to buy a Christmas tree. Besides, money was hard to find; so the Indians solved their problem by chopping down a palo verde in the nearby hills. The tree had sturdy branches and was just right for hanging the many varieties of gifts the Pimas brought in from their farms. I remember how a smart aleck put a little bird in a shoe box and hung it on the tree. When the box was opened, the birdie flew up to the ceiling. We children all laughed, but the adults did not find it so funny.

Oldham Eschief and his wife Laura, faithful Christians and translators of the hymns, had taught some of the mothers a Christmas song, which they sang after dinner, using appropriate gestures and clapping. Everyone enjoyed the performance, but some of the husbands made fun of their wives, saying, "Hmmm, the women act like they are killing mosquitoes!"

When the women were finished, some of the children gave recitations and sang songs. Finally, just as mother had promised, in came Santa Claus with a pack on his back. He amused the older children, but we little ones were frightened, and cries were heard. Later, when the children were older, some one hollered out, "Aw, we know Santa Claus is fat Louis!"

That year each girl received a rubber ball, and every boy got a bag of marbles. They were satisfied. Today the children receive too many gifts. Back then we enjoyed our most simple of festivities, for we loved the Lord Jesus, who had been born in a manger.

*   *   *

After Christmas my many long days of waiting for my brother Willie came to an end. I was enrolled in the little day school, and soon I was learning the three R's. Although I did not have him as a teacher long, I missed Hugh Patton when he left us. Mr. Patton was a Pima, and he taught in our native language. His wife, also a Pima, was house-keeper and nurse. Besides keeping the schoolhouse clean, she combed our hair to catch the lice and taught our mothers to make dresses for us. On the first day of enroll-ment, she issued a comb and a hairbrush to each of us.

This part of my early school days is dreamlike and hazy. I was afraid of the new non-Indian teacher. His commanding voice and his long stick scared the younger children. It was hard for us to understand the strange sounds of the English language he spoke. An older student named William Harrison was the interpreter for the white teacher. His nickname was *Kohji* (Hog), although I don't know why, for he was not fat but very skinny.

One day the new teacher whipped my cousin Steve, for what reason I do not remember. But I do remember that I cried along with my cousin. The teacher probably wondered why I was crying too, but it was the first time I'd seen someone get a whipping. In those days Indian parents never used a whip on their children. Instead they gave strong lectures on behavior, which ended with the oft-repeated words, "It is wrong, very wrong, to steal or disobey."

I received such lectures frequently. My parents were continually trying to instill in me the important Indian values which they had learned from their parents.

To teach me industry, mother made me a cute little olla in which I could carry water from the brook. It was decorated with Indian designs. "Stiffen your neck and walk straight, Annie," mother would tell me over and over. I tried, but it was so hard not to spill the water!

At first I was proud to use my little olla, but soon I grew lazy. One noon my nephew Harry and I were playing tag. He was chasing me around the olas kih when mother called, "Annie, take your olla and bring some fresh water for coffee-making!" Irritated because I had to stop my play, I picked up the little olla and set it down rather roughly, breaking its bottom. Then I began to cry.

Tell-tale Harry called, *"Lu-lu'u* (grandmother), Annie broke her olla on purpose!"

"Rub the broken piece of the olla on Annie's leg, or else the evil spirits will make her break another one!" shouted my brother Willie.

I cried louder. Mother, now a Christian, no longer believed in the old superstitions. She only looked at me sadly and said not a word. That hurt me more than a scolding. Today I can still feel the shame for that little broken olla.

Mother's nimble fingers were always busy, cooking, sewing, and weaving beautiful baskets. I tried to follow her ways and never be idle. She taught me to weave baskets to learn patience, but this tedious work seemed so difficult for a child! She also taught me to grind corn and roasted wheat for pinole, and to grind hard, unroasted wheat for Indian bread. But I would complain about the tough work. I can still hear my mother's patient voice saying, "My daughter, you must learn to grind the wheat for tortillas to feed your family when you are married."

"But we are going to eat the mil-gahn bread," I would retort.

"Your husband might be lazy and will not have money, so, my daughter, you must learn to grind wheat on the stone grinder." Ah, the bruised hands and sore knees! For the grinder must kneel down in order to properly grind the wheat.

To teach me to love dumb animals and not to be lazy,

my parents gave me pets to care for. I had cats, dogs, a goat, and a burro. I remember when my father brought my little burro home from the Papago country. "Annie," he said, "this burro is yours."

I lisped happily, *"T-kehg ni-wuhloga!* (pretty burro!)"

"You call that donkey pretty!" said Willie, and they all laughed.

Today as I look back on those childhood pets and remember my mother's patient lessons, I understand the reasons behind all these things. My parents so fervently hoped that we would learn the good Indian values which the ancient people had taught their children from one generation to the next. But how they also hoped that we would learn the ways of the mil-gahn! I still remember my mother sitting at the end of my grass mat late at night, praying to God to help her children to go to school and learn about the white man's world. She desired this more than anything, for she knew it would mean a livelihood for us.

Mother wanted so much for her children, and I'm afraid I must have disappointed her often. Being the youngest in the family, I was often spoiled and petted. Sometimes I refused to eat the pinole my poor mother so patiently ground and roasted, so she would shape it into little animals to make it more appealing. I'm afraid that many a little pinole coyote, dove, and pony ended up in the bushes around our olas kih! I just thought it was too chewy and hard to eat. Now I will travel miles to get pinole!

But mother wasn't the only one who spoiled me. My older brothers and sisters also gave in to my desires whenever they could afford to. Once I begged and cried to be allowed to see a circus parade in Phoenix. My elder brother Newton was going to town to buy groceries, so he told mother, "Let little sister go with me. I'll take care of her." Newton was married and had a child who was two or three years younger than I.

When the day came, mother awakened me at dawn. Quickly I jumped up from my grass mat. Soon we were on the road. It seemed a long, long time before we reached Phoenix.

I well remember standing on the curb with my brother, staring at the elephants, camels, and painted white ladies. The Indians called the elephants "crooked mouths" and the camels "humpbacks." How happy I was to see so many strange animals! I remember one of my married sisters saying to me, "Annie, don't *wuhi chesh* (eyes filled; don't get your eyes filled with so much excitement)."

*   *   *

My older brothers and sisters were always kind to me. And I enjoyed playing house and dolls with their babies and young children. The old Pimas called a babysitter like me *chukugshwad* (cricket). We did not rub our legs together to chirp lullabies, but we did like to sing and hum to put the little ones to sleep, so maybe that was how we got our name. The lullaby I liked most to sing went something like this:

Chuk mo'okam gihsob, ku'imediga chulachga
wuhpui kokosima. Biu, biu, biu!

In English the words would be something like this:

> Black-headed hummingbird, come to baby boy's
> eyes and cause him to sleep. Biu, biu, biu!

As a cricket I would rock the cradleboard or swing to and fro the hammocklike cradle, singing this lullaby. Of course, as with any child, laziness or desire to play would overwhelm me, and I would leave my sleeping nephew or niece, letting my maternal grandmother Song Endings take over the role of cricket.

Then I would race to the Gila River to join my brother and cousins — Willie, Steve, Clark, and Harry — in fishing, swimming, or playing tag high in the tall trees that grew along the riverbank. "Don't climb trees or you'll break your neck!" mother would warn us. But when she was not with us, we would climb the trees.

Tag was played in the water, too. This was hard for me because my brother was long-winded and could swim underwater for a long distance.

When I had tired of play, I would run back home, happy to relieve my grandmother of her small charges once more. Often this sweet and patient old one would tell us stories of the past and relate tribal legends as we rested at her feet. She had seen the falling of the stars in 1833. These meteoric showers were recorded both on the Pima calendar stick and in the white man's history books.

Of this event, Grandmother Song Endings would tell us: "The world now is in good condition. But when the stars went loco and were flying around, we were scared. Some people thought our gods were angry for some wrong we had committed. Other people thought the medicine men had caused the catastrophe to show their power."

"Please, grandmother, tell us a story of what it was like to live before Christianity was brought to the Indians," we would coax. And she would patiently begin:

"Back in the old days when Phoenix was just a small town, the Pimas would go there to sell their artifacts and buy a few groceries for their families. But the pioneer settlers could not stand the sight of naked Indians. Oh no! Too obnoxious!

"Finally a city ordinance was made. Hereafter, the Indians must wear trousers or be thrown in jail for indecent exposure. An interpreter told the Pimas about their misfortune: 'You must wear white man's clothes or be arrested and thrown in jail.'

" *'Tt has wo t-juh?* (What shall we do?)' cried the men, for money was scarce. They needed to sell their handicrafts to buy food.

"Then a young brave had a bright idea. 'I know! Let's buy one or two overalls. Then we'll take turns wearing them into town!' A basket was passed around and each person threw in his few coins. Soon there was enough for the purchase of two pairs of overalls.

"It so happened that there was a mesquite thicket nearby, not chopped down by the white man's ax. This chaparral was near the city, and it was just the right spot for the Indians to change their clothes. Children, can't you see the Pimas going back and forth, like ants storing up food? When it was evening and all had bought their groceries, they rolled up their overalls and safely hid them in the thorny branches of the mesquite. Then they mounted their ponies and started for home, loaded down with good food for their families.

"Their dusty trail led them by *Babath Thak* (Sitting Frog), a large boulder that resembles a frog and so has that name. They also passed *Waw Thadha* (Sitting Cliffs), located in the Papago Park as we now know it.

"The Pima braves were laughing at jokes, yelling, and singing, breaking the evening stillness. If the whites only knew of the trick they had used! It was a red letter day when the Pimas solved their problem with their ingenuity."

*   *   *

Of all Grandmother Song Endings' stories, my favorite was one of the oldest — the legend of Ho'ok, the ugly old witch. Over and over we would ask her to tell us this legend, and she would patiently begin the tale once more:

"The old witch lived in a mountain cave. She was ugly. Her fingers were like claws. She would come to the Indian village to grab newborn babies. Her rough voice was disguised, and when she wanted her prey she would use her sweet smiles and charms and ask, '*Chu Mohmsi* (my grandchildren), let me hold the baby in my arms.' The mothers would see her sharp claws, but they were under her power, so they always obeyed Ho'ok. When she got her way, she would kick up her heels and flee to the cave with the infant. The distressed parents were left wailing for their little one.

"The inhabitants tried various ways to keep the witch away from the village, but she was very powerful. Their plans were always thwarted.

"In desperation, they called on a wise man named Elder Brother, who lived in Greasy Mountain. The people asked him to help them get rid of Ho'ok. Elder Brother was angered at the witch's deeds and said, 'I will help you. Return to your village and gather dry mesquite wood and place it in a cave. In four days, we should have everything ready. Tell the witch to join us in a circle dance.'

"The next four days were busy ones. Dry wood was stacked in a cave that was located somewhere in the vast desert hills. Tohono O'othham, our cousins, the Papagos, were invited to the dance. During the four days, excitement mixed with anxiety was felt by the Indians.

"Using his metate, Elder Brother finely crushed *jewed heosig* (earth flowers), which were very powerful but had a sweet aroma. He mixed the potent earth flowers with tobacco. This was to be used to charm the witch.

"The day of the Circle Dance finally came. Singers sat on the ground and beat on turned-over, large, handwoven baskets, a signal the dance was to begin. Ho'ok heard and came at once. She wore her necklace of dried white bones, which made a weird rattling sound when she danced. Elder Brother gave her tobacco to smoke. 'Chu mohmsi!' she exclaimed and puffed on the tobacco. After dancing awhile, she fell in a heap, muttering 'Chu mohmsi, my grandchildren!'

"Now Elder Brother was a little man but so very strong. He carried the old witch on his back to the cave, her feet dragging and making marks on the ground. He dumped her among the wood and, with his tobacco stub, lit the fire. Before long the cave was aglow. Sharp cries were heard from inside the hot cave. But Elder Brother had power to keep Ho'ok inside her hot cage.

Suddenly a loud crack like thunder was heard. Once again, fear crept into the hearts of the ancient River People. But Elder Brother knew what to do. You see, he had power too. He quickly climbed on top of the hill, and when he found the cracked rock he stepped on it and closed it for all time.

"The people were relieved and so very happy. Clearing their throats, they sang, *'Ho'ok mehitha, Ho'ok mehitha!* (witch burning!)' "

When she had finished this legend, grandmother would always add: "It is claimed that Elder Brother's footprint is still visible on the cracked rock. But children, do not go looking for this sign! You might get lost in the desert!"

*   *   *

How well I remember Grandmother Song Endings' gentle warnings! How can any of her many grandchildren ever forget her sweet disposition? Her seven children respected and loved her. When she became a Christian she was given the name of Mrs. Rebecca Rovie.

I am fortunate to have my grandmother's little grinding stone, which was buried on the farm after her death. It came to light due to frequent plowings of the field. I treasure it in my Indian collection. That grinding stone once nourished me with ground *poshol* (succotash). We children would sit beside grandmother while she rolled the mano over the cooked wheat and brown beans . . . very delicious.

Grandmother Song Endings lived with us for some years before she passed away at the age of one hundred years.

She is the only grandparent I remember. My maternal Grandfather Black Shirt went to Morning Land when I was only three or four years old. I remember the night well. My father and I were walking hand-in-hand toward the knoll where my maternal grandparents lived. In the stillness of the night, I heard the cries of people.

"Kai! (hear!)" I said in my squeaky childish voice.

My maghm gently answered, "Yes, Chehia, your *bahb* (grandfather) has left us for Si'al Wui."

When I grew older, I learned that Grandfather Black Shirt had been a great warrior. Once he had laughingly told his family this story about the time he went to make peace with the Yumas:

"The soldiers stopped a short distance and through an interpreter told us, 'Rather than to be seen with you, we will remain here. It will be better for you scouts to go alone. The Yumas might think we are going to fight and start trouble. We will come to help you should they start a fight.'

"When we arrived, we found the Yuma Indians sitting on the ground waiting for us. One big Yuma man came to me and fell at my feet. 'My friend Black Shirt, I have been waiting for you! We heard you were coming.'

"My heart seemed to be in my throat ready to jump out. I thought he was going to kill me — but the man had taken too much firewater, and his legs stumbled!

"The Yumas had grown weary of the war trails, and they willingly accepted the peace treaty. The white soldiers spoke to the group of Pimas and Yumas. We all gave grunts of approval, thus ending the feuds of long standing."

Black Shirt did not live to become a Christian. My father's generation was the first to be converted. Ours was the first to be educated in two cultures, the Pima and the white. Sometimes the values of the two were in conflict, but we were learning to put them together to make a way of life different from anything the early Pimas ever dreamed of.

More Twofold Learning

THE RESERVATION SCHOOL and family life were central forces in my childhood training. But I would be remiss to leave out another important influence — the little adobe house of God. Every Sunday my family joined the throng of Pimas who marched to the service in their best clothes.

As a child, I thought the long sermons were very boring, even though in those days we little ones were allowed to eat in church so we wouldn't fall asleep. Next to the hymns, I most liked the antics of four flashy young braves who always filed into the church after everyone else was seated. Wearing their chaps and spurs, they would sit on the last bench in the rear. Whenever the message seemed to point at their wayward deeds, they would stalk out of the room, their spurs jingling.

In later years all of these men were converted, and one of them was enrolled at the C. H. Cook Christian Training School. After graduation he went south to expound the Good News to the Papagos. Upon his retirement, Herbert Grant returned to Phoenix, where he served as director of the Phoenix Indian Center. But despite his ultimate reformation, I still fondly remember Herb as one of those dashing young rebels who entertained me during those long, long sermons.

The teenaged ones in those days were also in their glory, playing tricks on the early Christians. The oldsters' dignities were disturbed when they left the service and found their saddles turned around, while snickering boys could be heard nearby. On pitch-dark nights a family would sometimes discover that a wheel on their wagon had been mysteriously loosened.

The teenagers didn't mean to be bad but were just full of fun. As they grew up they came to appreciate the meaning of the Bible message they were so constantly exposed to.

I also was beginning to appreciate the meaning of the Gospel. Despite my being bored during the sermons, the good words rubbed off on me. Even as a little child I learned to love Jesus and tried to practice the Golden Rule. But sometimes I envied the old way of life, when Pima children didn't have to go to school and could look forward to colorful tribal dances and festivals.

Now, under the influence of the missionaries, the old Indian dances were dying out. I would have no puberty ceremonial, and Circle and Name-Calling dances were almost things of the past. When grandmother would tell me of an old festival like the Ho'ok, or Witch-Burning ceremony, I would wish I had been born in the days gone by.

Once father must have sensed my curiosity regarding the ancient traditions. He called my brother and me to him and said, "Willie and Annie, you must always remember that the white *pahl* (preacher) has said that the tribal dances and the festivals at Saint John's Mission are not for Christians to attend. Those who go to these events are sinners. The devil will get them. Remember this, my children."

Father's words were stern, but I noticed that he had not literally forbidden us to go. I resolved that when he was not with me I would sneak off and see a dance or two. I was curious!

As it happened I had no chance to attend a tribal ceremony at that time. However, on June 24, San Juan's Day, my girlfriend and I sneaked away to the little Catholic mission, where the courtyard was alive with dancing and singing. There were good spicy smells of tamales, tacos, enchiladas, and bean burros. We sat and ate the delicious food while we watched the chicken-pulling contest. Men tried to grab a rooster off the ground as they rode by on their ponies. How strange that seemed to me! How sorry I felt for the poor little chicken!

I don't know if father ever knew about my attending that first fiesta, but later, when he was an ordained elder of the church, he was embarrassed by my behavior. While he was questioning a local girl about her attendance at some Saint John's event, a man said to him, "Question thyself! What was your Annie doing there, Josiah?" After that I stayed away from the forbidden festivals.

*   *   *

I never thought of it then, but giving up the tribal ways must have been even harder for my parents, who had been raised in the old traditions. One event in particular shows how my mother must have been torn between the two sets of beliefs.

One morning when I was dressing for school, I told my mother that during the night I had dreamed that my little niece Margaret had died. Mother looked worried and said to me, "In the old days many Pimas dreamed things that would come true, Annie. Your dream is not good, for I, too, have had a bad sign this morning. The hen who had laid her eggs here in the house began to crow like a rooster. Before we were Christians we would wring its neck to prevent the bad luck it might bring. Today I just shooed it out of doors."

I thought no more about my dream and the crowing hen during my busy day at school. But when I got home, I was surprised to find that my little niece was pale. Mother told me I couldn't play dolls with her, for she had diarrhea. A week later she passed away.

After the funeral I could tell that mother was troubled by the event. Even though she no longer believed in the old superstitions, she wondered if Margaret would have lived if she had killed the crowing chicken. She was torn between two worlds.

Other Pimas in her generation had the same problem. They would especially question the white man's ways when they experienced misfortune because of them. One year the agent prohibited the Indians from selling wood to the pioneer settlers of Phoenix and Tempe. The Pimas badly need the money for food. I remember hearing the older people talk about starvation. Some of them wanted to take up their weapons and go on the war trail to remedy the situation. But the rule was lifted, and all was peaceful again.

*   *   *

My brother Willie was now nine years old. I guess he felt grown up and wanted to get away from our parents' rule, for he asked to attend the Tucson Indian Mission School, established for the Pima and Papago tribes by the Presbyterian Board of Home Missions. Our own Dr. Cook had instigated the building of this school, so my parents were moved to comply with Willie's wishes. How I missed my brother that first year he was away at boarding school!

Finally summer vacation came. But Willie decided that instead of coming straight home, he would get off the Southern Pacific with a friend who lived in Sacaton. Father was desperate when Willie did not show up at the depot! He rode his pony to Wa'akih to ask after his son. When he failed to find him there, he went on to Sacaton. There he found Willie playing marbles with his friend Alfred. When Willie finally came home, he was meek as a lamb. Father had given him a strong talk about his conduct.

Not long daunted, Willie was soon filling my eager ears with stories of life at boarding school. Once he told me about a big wheel that turned round and round. He had never seen such a large wheel.

"Was it like a wagon wheel?" I asked.

"Yes, Annie, but much bigger than a wagon wheel."

"If such a wheel is in Tucson, I would like to go with you, Willie, to the mission school to see it."

Mother and father agreed to let me go away to boarding school with my brother that fall, although for reasons other than allowing me to see the wondrous wheel. So in September 1906 our family put food and bedding in the wagon and set out for Sacaton.

School officials demanded that new students have a physical examination before enrollment at the Tucson Indian Mission. At first I was afraid of the white doctors with their strange shiny instruments, but then I saw Dr. Clarence Ellis, the missionary from Gila Crossing who had attended Juana. I felt better when I found this familiar face. I felt proud when I heard him tell the other doctors, "Her father, Josiah Moore, is an ordained elder of the Gila Crossing Mission." I was relieved when I passed the physical.

After the ordeal, mother took me to see my *wihkol* (a distant relative on the mother's side). The great Pima chief Antonio Azul, now very old and wrinkled, lived in a two-story adobe house. I remember him asking mother, "Is Annie old enough to go away to school?" This was the last time I saw my veecol. His Pima name was *Mawith Kawdan* (Lion Shield).

Late that afternoon we hitched up the wagon and headed for *Hanamkam* (Cholla Bud Town, the Indian name for Casa Grande). We camped on the outskirts of the settlement, and the campfires glowed as the good smell of fried bread filled the night air.

The next morning before dawn, an Indian policeman went to every camp to tell the parents to awaken their children. The train from the west would arrive pronto. The children must be at the tracks waiting to board it.

Mother dressed me in my best clothes, then braided my long hair and tied it with pink ribbons. As we ate our beans and tortillas I began to tremble with fear, for I was only eight years old and had never been away from my parents before.

After breakfast we walked to meet the train. The puffing smoke and loud whistle scared me. To what sort of ugly place would this monstrous iron wagon take me? I thought I might cry as I waved goodbye to my mother and father.

Soon the big wagon was rolling along, picking up speed while we children looked through the windows at the desert scenery. We began to forget our fears as we giggled to see the cacti and desert bushes flying by before our eyes.

My brother Willie sat with his school friends, who were busily talking about their happy summers. They compared the numbers of rabbit and quail they had shot and talked of the threshing and other farm work they had done to help their parents. I did not miss Willie's attention because I soon made friends with a little girl with short hair named May Enos. She told me, "Ann, you are going to like the mission school. It is a very good school. The teachers are nice."

I thought of the time my cousin was whipped at the reservation day school and answered, "I know I'll like the school, but do the children get whipped?"

"When they are naughty," she replied. "When we get there, I'll take you around the buildings." Off and on during the trip my little friend talked to keep me from getting homesick. At once I liked her very much.

The train finally slowed down and stopped. We followed the older ones on the walk to the mission school, near where the University of Arizona stands today. The first thing I saw there was a high fence surrounding immense, tall buildings. It was not until much later that I saw the wonderful water wheel which had prompted me to come to Tucson.

My new friend and I were assigned to an upstairs dorm. I had never climbed a stairway before. In the dorm a row of single beds stood side by side. "Oh, this is going to be fun!" I thought. "Imagine sleeping on a real bed with other girls my age!" At home we had lived too far from my schoolmates for me to play with them every day. Now I would have friends around me all the time!

The matron told us all to take showers before we went to the dining room. I wondered about taking a shower. What did that word mean? My little friend showed me where the shower rooms were. Then she took me to the dining room. It was such a huge room, with long tables and an aisle between the girls' tables and the boys'.

All the little girls sat at one long table with an older girl as monitor at the head. She helped us to learn table manners and dished out the food for us. Before we sat down to eat, we repeated the Grace in unison.

Some of the most exciting events at school were my first meals there. The cornflakes which I ate for breakfast were delicious, and I never knew how or of what they were made.

On Saturdays we shined the silverware with brick dust, for Sunday was a special day, and everything must be clean and shiny. A big girl named Mary Williams was our boss. She was very kind to us and was not strict even if our work was not well done.

On Mondays through Fridays we marched to our classrooms to study Bible verses, reading, and spelling. I do not remember if we were taught arithmetic; it was always a dull subject for me.

Of all our studies, I most enjoyed the lessons from the Good Book. I especially liked memorizing verses from the Gospels: they have been a spiritual blessing all my life and have helped me handle many hard knocks. My favorite verse was Matthew 24:35: "Heaven and earth shall pass away, but my words shall not pass away."

The teacher was a kind person. She had been to the Orient and could tell many interesting tales about Japan. Often she placed her souvenirs from that far-away land on a table for us to inspect and touch — a beautiful parasol, kites, seashells, and fine silk.

We were not allowed to speak the Pima tongue at school. Some students would report on those who spoke in Indian, and as punishment our mouths would be taped. We did not mind, for the matron, teachers, and other employees were good to us despite our naughty ways.

In the winter our hands became chapped and painful. Instead of the *ko'owi gihgi* (rattlesnake fat) or Vaseline that mother had used, they gave us a can of lard for our hands. I later learned that the school was doing its best on a very slim budget.

Our clothes were hand-me-downs, but the shoes were new. A friend and I one day sat under a tree, trying to put holes in our shoes. For some reason we didn't like our shoes and thought if we could punch holes in them we would each be given another pair. What crazy ideas young children can make up! It was a good thing we were not strong enough to damage our shoes.

One Saturday we were taken to a football game between the Indians and a white team. I stood with the girls and watched with tears in my eyes. I couldn't understand this strange new sport and wondered why my cousin Lewis and his teammates were being shoved and pushed around, sometimes getting up with their faces all smeared with dirt. Later I learned that the roughness was all in fun.

We little girls played the much tamer game of jacks, using smooth round pebbles. I had never played jacks before, but I soon learned the game. Some of us would play for a long time after we had shined the silverware. Mary, our boss, inspected our work before we could play.

One evening after supper when we were playing jacks, we saw some Indian men coming to the school. We stopped our game to watch them. Then I saw my brother Willie and the other boys running to meet the visitors. Suddenly I recognized my brother J. Newton! I was so surprised, for I had never dreamed I would ever see anyone from home here at school. "Father was not able to make the trip," explained Newton.

The men brought us flour sacks filled with Indian food. There were Indian beans wrapped in fried bread, pinole, and tortillas. How delicious the old tastes seemed after so many months of eating the white man's food!

I didn't understand how the Pimas had made the trip to Tucson, but I was too bashful to ask questions. After I returned home for summer vacation, I asked mother about the visit. She explained how the white chief in Washington had given permission to the Pimas to ride the freight trains free. But some of the Indians abused this privilege and drank too much vino. This caused accidents, so the rides were discontinued to safeguard Indian lives.

*   *   *

Christmas came, and we were awakened by beautiful carols sung by the older girls. How surprised I was to receive many toys! I was especially thrilled with a beautiful china doll with brown hair and eyes to match. I loved her so! At home I had been used to playing with mud dolls, rag dolls, and even pig's knuckles that I wrapped with a red cloth to make them beautiful. My parents could not afford store toys for us. But now I had this wonderful china dollie!

All Christmas day I played dolls with the other little girls. How I longed to do nothing but play house like that every day! I remember asking a foolish question: "Why do we have to go to school?"

"To learn to speak English, that's why," explained our silver-cleaning boss Mary.

Reluctantly we replaced our dolls in trunks that had rounded, convex tops that looked like the backs of turtles. But we still played house with our dollies whenever we could.

Some of my friends had been telling me that snow always fell on New Year's day. I looked forward to it, since I had never seen snow in all my life. When the day came and brought no snow, I was disappointed.

*　　*　　*

One other event of that school year I will never forget was Washington's birthday celebration. Our third grade teacher planned a special program. My cousin George, the brother of Lewis the football player, was chosen to take the role of George Washington. A suit and a wig were made for him, and he rehearsed what he should do and say. My little friend Lucille was Martha Washington. She wore a beautiful white crepe-paper dress with pink roses painted on it, and I was chosen to follow her to take care of her long train.

The day came, and the room was crowded with older students waiting for the show to begin. What a program it was! We participants were stage-struck and tongue-tied. George Washington's wig dropped on the floor. I stepped on Martha Washington's long train and tore it. What a mess we made of our teacher's careful plans!

That evening, when we were in line to go to the dining room, I was told to get out of the line and go back to the Girls' Building.

"You are punished for talking during the pageant. No supper!" said Mr. Pablo, the Papago Indian who was in charge.

I hung my head in shame and left the line. Footsteps sounded behind me, and I saw my friend Lucille following me. "How come your uncle, Mr. Pablo, punished you too? It was all my fault, not yours."

"No, I am to blame too. I laughed out loud when you called me Mrs. George Washington," answered Lucille.

We did not mind going without supper. Of course we felt guilty for our misconduct, but to forget it we played jacks. That was the only time I was punished in this manner at the mission school. Our teachers and matrons were very good to us.

*   *   *

When summer vacation time finally arrived, everyone was anxious to return to their respective reservations, the

Papagos to the desert country, and the Pimas to the Salt and Gila rivers. How good it was to see my parents and all my beloved little nieces and nephews! We so much enjoyed the goodtimes of summer that we weren't really disappointed when fall arrived and our father could not afford to pay the ten-dollar railroad fare to Tucson that was now required.

We stayed home and pretended that we were too old to go to school. But our freedom was not to last for long. One Sunday Mr. Campbell, the Gila Crossing Day School teacher, saw us at church. He immediately asked the attendance officer to take us to school the following day. "They are both too young to end their educations," he told our parents.

So once again Willie and I could be seen trudging daily to the little adobe school house on the knoll. We were both placed in the fourth grade, the highest one in the school.

We children called the teacher *Com-la,* as Campbell was too hard to pronounce properly. I remember him asking us to stand in front of the class to read from the fourth-grade reader. If we did not speak loud enough, he would remind us, "The classrooms at the Phoenix Indian School are large, so speak louder and be heard. I want all my students to make good." We would clear our throats and start all over, almost shouting.

Mr. Campbell's daughter Gertrude taught our Sunday school class. We memorized the names of the books in the New Testament, and I was her helper, interpreting for some of the students who didn't know English. I guess my schooling was finally paying off in some small mastery of the white man's language.

*   *   *

On September 1, 1908, my brother and I enrolled at the government boarding school in Phoenix. I had never had money to spend and was afraid to take the bright shiny dollar my father offered me. Instead I accepted a thin dime. Now wasn't I the silly one! I was only ten years old and still quite shy and innocent.

At first I was homesick and lonesome for my parents and my little nieces and nephews. I was beginning to appreciate my humble home. I would picture my mother making tortillas or fried bread for breakfast. She was so capable and kind and loving! Remorse would overcome me when I thought of some of my past uncalled-for actions, and I would begin to cry. I had never cried with homesickness at the Tucson Indian Mission School. I guess that at last I was beginning to grow up and develop some common sense.

I always went home to the reservation for summer vacations, of course. Then each fall I would be homesick again, although never so badly as during that first year. Once when I was fourteen the matron showed me a Phoenix newspaper which had a picture of J. Newton's little son Russell Moore. His parents had entered him in the well-baby contest at the Sacaton fair, and he had won first prize. The paper described him as an "Adonis." Even though by this time I was used to being away at school, I couldn't help but shed a few tears at seeing the picture. I had taken care of Russell, and I missed him and my other little charges.

But it was only natural for me to be homesick. The strictly regulated life we led at school was so different from the freedom of the reservation. You see, in those early days the Phoenix Indian School was a semi-military institution. They had a boys' and a girls' battalion, called the First and Second battalions respectively. The companies were named alphabetically from A to F, and I was placed in the E Company.

The students were taught to keep in step to the music of the school band. When we went to the bean hall, or dining room, we marched to a military tune. A snare drummer always beat his rhythms in front of the academic building, and we had to keep in step.

At first the marching seemed so hard to learn, but once we had mastered the knack, we couldn't break the habit. Sometimes on our once-a-month visit to town, a talking machine would be blasting band music outside a store to attract customers. Then we girls would go into our act; try as hard as we could, we just couldn't get out of step. It was impossible! We'd try to take long strides to break the rhythm, but soon we would fall back into step again. How embarrassing it was!

Our company's captain was a Pima girl and a very good leader. She would drill us every morning at 5:00 A.M. in preparation for the annual state fair. The boys' and girls' battalions always had a place on the fair's Indian Day program. We would pass in review, and one could hear the captain's commands: "Company, march! Left, right, left, right!" Then suddenly, "Company, halt!" When the battalions were all lined up, the famous Indian School Band with Peter A. Venne as band master would commence to march to rousing Sousa compositions. The boy and girl majors would have to shout in order to be heard: "Pass in review!" And we would march proudly by the big grandstand. The loud clapping by the non-Indian spectators rewarded us for our efforts.

On days like that I had more reason than most to be proud: my brother Willie, whom we now called Bill, was one of the outstanding members of the marching band. Already his unusual musical abilities had come to the fore, and Mr. Venne had taught him to play several instruments, with concentration on the baritone horn.

Bill had plenty of opportunities to show off, for the band, along with the First and Second battalions, performed during every important event at the school. I recall the day President William Howard Taft visited us in 1910. We marched with the band to the place he was to speak, in front of the Girls' Building. I don't know what the president said, but I do recall that Grace McAfee, a little Pima girl from the Salt River Reservation, presented him with a bouquet of red roses. One confused Pima lad whispered, "Gee! George Washington is fat!"

When Arizona became a state on February 14, 1912, we Indian students followed the band through the streets of Phoenix, with the First Battalion leading and the Second following. When we returned to the school, we exhausted girls immediately fell asleep on our beds. We slept all afternoon until the 5:00 P.M. whistle blew. I still remember the matron coming to awaken us in her shrill voice: "Girls! girls! It's time to go to supper!"

*   *   *

The matron's bunch of jingling keys always warned us of her presence. She was strict and frequently used her strap on us. We did not understand this punishment at the time; we just assumed that she was mean like a witch. In fact, we girls gave her the nickname Ho'ok after the wicked old witch in the Pima legend. We used this name to signal that she was coming into the dorm to make sure we were in our beds. I can still hear my friends frantically whispering, "Ho'ok! Ho'ok!" Then we would jump into our beds and pretend that we were sound asleep in order to escape the strap.

Mary, a tall slender girl, used to imitate the matron in fun. She tied some large nails together so they would jingle like old Ho'ok's keys. Then she would call out in a nasal tone, "Girls! girls!" How she giggled when she saw us scattering in every direction like scared rabbits!

How Mary came to be enrolled at the Indian School we never knew as she, her sister, and her brother were non-Indians. The school also had many Mexican-American boys and girls, who were later sent to another institution. For the most part we students were Arizona Indians, but there were also representatives of tribes from Oklahoma, the Dakotas, and California. Together we were one big happy family.

A system was set up to give us the opportunity to learn the various trades: home economics, dressmaking, carpentry, plumbing, nursing, and such. We were scheduled to work at our trade half the day and spend the other half at our academic studies.

I first learned how to darn stockings. Then I worked in the dining room, washing dishes and scrubbing floors. My little helpers and I hadn't even reached our teen-aged years yet, and this work seemed so hard! If we were not finished when the 8:00 A.M. whistle sounded, the dining room matron would go around strapping us while we were still on our hands and knees. This was just the right position for a swat — all the matron had to do was raise our dresses and strap.

The bakery was next to the dining room, and the bakery boys loved to see us get a strapping; they would always stare and grin. The matron was really trying to teach us a lesson on how to work steadily and get our jobs done on time, but we didn't understand at that early age. We just dreaded the sore bottoms! The matron previous to this one had been a Pima named Nellie Santeo. We had obeyed her willingly, even though she was kind and didn't use a strap.

Every quarter work assignments were changed. I longed to be transferred from the dining room, but it was my lot to remain there for two long years. Finally I was delighted to find I'd been assigned to the laundry, where we ironed the school clothes and bedding. That was not so bad as the dining room work, but my favorite trade training was in domestic science and art, to which I was transferred during my last years at the school. We made pastries and prepared luncheons for our teachers and friends. We also learned to crochet, knit, and sew. I remember making my own eighth-grade graduation dress and blue serge coat. My serge coat was made into a little boy's coat after I left the school.

Childhood Sweethearts

ALTHOUGH THE GIRLS AND BOYS were strictly separated at the Phoenix Indian School, we could not help but notice each other. This was especially true as we became teenagers and young adults. You see, in those days most of us spent two years in each grade in order to master the difficult English language along with the subject matter. Indian students most often would be from eighteen to twenty-two when they graduated from eighth grade, old enough for marriage.

The first and only romance of my life began in 1912 when I was fourteen years old. I no longer wore my hair in pigtails, and the attentions of a handsome Pima named Ross Shaw were flattering. We wrote notes because the matron was very strict and only let us see each other at social functions. But sometimes Ross would sneak over to the girls' side of the campus, where we would play croquet until the matron discovered us and shooed Ross back where he belonged. Soon we were going together. We were truly childhood sweethearts.

*   *   *

Our backgrounds were very similar, but Ross' family was even more traditional than mine. Born on the Salt

All spruced up for a date with Ross, I seem pretty proud of my new dress, one of the products of the Indian School sewing class. Our dates were very different from those of modern teenagers, for back then the school was quite strict. We were only allowed to see each other once a week, at chaperoned parties in the girls' sitting room on Saturday nights. They never even let us hold hands!

Ross was an athlete as well as a good student. He marched as an adjutant in the First Battalion and played a good game of football. Once he beat an Apache boy in a track-meet dash, much to the delight of us Indians from other tribes. We were so tired of hearing the Apaches brag about their running ability!

River Reservation in 1892, he was named *Jujul Tonol* (Zigzag Light). When he entered day school, the teacher thought he seemed about eight years old and recorded his age as such. Actually he was ten, but those two years the teacher chopped off his age have appeared on every document concerning Ross ever since.

The teacher also made another mistake; when she named Ross and the little boy in line behind him, she didn't realize that they were brothers. Ross chuckles when he tells about it: "You be Ross Shaw and you be Paul Jones," she told them. Confused and without a knowledge of English, the two brothers could not object and were stuck with the different surnames until 1910, when they received their land allotments from the BIA.

Ross' father, *Hudinig Shahmuni* (Evening Tranquility), bore the English name Jacob Step Shaw. He was a hard worker and a good provider for his seven children, the youngest of whom were twin boys. His wife Sihba, a beautiful part-Maricopa with a brilliant mind, was also a tireless worker. Nearly every morning she could be heard shouting the same words to her sleeping children: "Wake up, boys! Wake up! Maybe you think that you will get rest on this earth, but you are wrong. You never rest until you die."

Mother Shaw was Catholic in name only, for her large family left her little time for church-going. But nonetheless she wanted an education for her children, and she did everything she could to aid Ross in his struggle to go to school.

He spent two years at the Tucson Indian Mission. Then when he was fourteen he spent the summer riding a horse to pick cantaloupes in Mesa. The pay was $1.50 a day, which was big money then. Still, when fall came around Ross felt that his family could not afford the ten-dollar fare to Tucson, and he enrolled in the Phoenix Indian School. That was in 1907.

Ross was one grade higher than me for most of our years at the school, but in 1915 I received a double promotion, so we were in seventh grade together. Like all young lovers, we made plans. After we graduated from eighth grade, we both hoped to attend Phoenix Union High School. A football coach there had already asked Ross to play on the team. We planned to be married after we received our diplomas.

But who could foretell the future? Fate changed our well-laid plans. In the spring of 1916, just before we were to graduate, Pancho Villa, the Mexican guerrilla leader, raided Agua Prieta on the international boundary near Douglas, Arizona. National guardsmen were called in to stop further depredations, and Ross was one of them.

How well I remember the evening in May when he was called. Sergeant Joshua Morris came into the school dining room and picked out the members who were to go. Ross walked out of the dining room and out of my day-to-day life for three long years.

*   *   *

I had to begin my high school education without my fiancé. Of course I saw him on occasional leaves, but these were few and far between. My brother Bill was also gone, serving on the staff of an Indian school in Zuni, New Mexico. Later he volunteered to serve his country as a member of the 158th Infantry Indian Band.

But even though I was lonely for my men, I managed to keep busy. Bill faithfully sent me part of his paycheck each month, and I also took on the job of assistant seamstress at the Indian School, where I was given a small salary and room and board in exchange for my efforts.

Actually, I remained a student at the Indian School, even though I had graduated from eighth grade. With Ross gone I decided to take advantage of a new program which provided graduates with their first two years of high school. Thus it was not until my junior year that I finally entered Phoenix Union High.

Even after that I continued to work and live at the Phoenix Indian School. Each morning I would wait to board a trolley almost at the entrance of the campus. After a clanging and clacking ride through a Phoenix which looked very different from the modern city of today, I would arrive at high school to begin a day of classes.

I liked all my teachers and appreciated their special efforts to help me pass subjects which may have been a bit neglected in my education at the Indian School. A teacher named Miss Summers was my inspiration. She helped me learn American history and stressed the dates of important events, which I could not see the significance of at the time.

Unfortunately I had little time for extracurricular activities, for after school I had to board the trolley again in order to do my job at the Indian School and still have a few hours left for homework. I did find time to form a number of very dear friendships with non-Indian girls at Phoenix Union High, however. Besides these close chums, I had many other good acquaintances. In fact, throughout my days in high school I never noticed any prejudice directed at me because of my Indian blood. This was important, for my friendships did a lot to help me through that long period away from Ross.

My high school education meant a long time away from my family too. In that duration I was able to visit the reservation only once. Money was as scarce as hen's teeth during the war years, and I was saving every cent of my paycheck along with the money Bill sent me in order to continue my schooling on the university level.

To help me achieve this goal, Indian School Superintendent J. Brown arranged for me to keep house for a nice family called the Heflins in exchange for room and board. This freed me from the daily trolley rides and left me more time for studying.

As the time of Ross' return approached, however, my plans for a higher education began to lose their appeal. I was now twenty-one years old, and marriage and a family seemed more important to me than college books. After all, I had already been attending school for almost fifteen years! I told Bill to stop sending me money and began to look on my little savings as a nest egg for Ross' and my future.

*   *   *

While I was studying and waiting for Ross, my fiancé was busy fighting with Mexican guerrillas, protecting the American border. Those years must have been hard ones for him too, for he seldom saw the folks back home. I remember one time the Phoenix Indian School wanted to give their National Guard boys a special treat — five gallons of homemade ice cream. When the ice cream arrived at the border camp, Ross and his buddies had been transferred. The treat soon melted and spoiled, and how distressed we were! It had been the Indians' favorite flavor — fresh strawberry or *s-wegichu* (red).

When Ross finally returned after nearly two years of skirmishing along the border, he was faced with a difficult decision. The United States had declared war on Germany, but guardsmen of Indian descent were told they need not fight. "You are not citizens," their commander told them, "and therefore you are not eligible for the draft. However, those who want to fight may join the army of their own volition."

Quiet moments followed the announcement. Then Joshua Morris whispered to Ross, *"Tt wo hihim k wo cheggia!* (Let us go fight!)" As the two brave men stepped up to the desk, the other Indian soldiers who had no families to support also rose to their feet and walked up to volunteer. Patriots all, of their own free wills they decided to risk their lives for their native land, as had their ancestors.

The Indian Company F was in the 158th Infantry that included the famous band of which my brother Bill was a member. They received orders to go to Camp Kearney in San Diego, California, where they were assigned to the Fortieth Division, soon to be nicknamed the Sunshine Division. After Theda Bara, a beautiful vampire actress, visited the camp and announced that she considered herself their "godmother," the division came to be called the Vampire Regiment.

Because of the semi-military training the Indians had received at the BIA schools, they made a good record.

The 40th Division, 158th Infantry, posed for this picture just before they were sent overseas. The arrows point out the men mentioned in this book: in the back row (left to right) Sergeant Joshua Morris and Ross Shaw; in front my schoolmate Wallace Anton, my sister Juana's son Harry Lives, and my brother Bill Moore.

Thanks and much credit is due the BIA, for the boys were outstanding in marching, fighting, and trench warfare. They were also known for their hardiness; they could walk for miles without tiring when army trucks were not available. It is told how once on a walk to La Jolla a white soldier grew weary and ready to drop. One of the sturdy Pima boys helped him by carrying his heavy pack.

In August 1918 the Fortieth Division was ordered to board the train for an Eastern port, where camouflaged ships awaited to take them across the Atlantic. They landed in England, where they were welcomed heartily. Little urchins followed them on their march to temporary camp, picking up the coins the soldiers threw to them.

Some of the Company F men, including Ross, were sent on to Le Havre, France. The French were also very friendly, and soon the Indians had acquired a few words of the language in order to buy food. They learned to eat the strange long loaves of white bread and got used to the strong smells of wine and garlic in the restaurants.

My brother Bill was also in France, marching with the band. I kept myself busy sending hand-knit sweaters and socks to my loved ones in that faraway land. I also knitted warm things for the Red Cross to distribute to other fighting boys.

Naturally I spent a lot of time worrying about Ross and Bill. Ross' outfit was called to wait behind the battleline until they were needed. Just before they were to go to the front, the armistice was signed. My brother Bill also never reached the front line of battle, but the 158th Infantry Indian Band was chosen to play in Paris when Woodrow Wilson met with other world leaders to sign the armistice that brought to a close the War to End All Wars.

Some of our Indian boys were not so lucky as Ross and Bill. But in the midst of the heavy fighting they distinguished themselves by their bravery. Indeed, many of our Indian soldiers paid the supreme sacrifice, including Matthew B. Juan of Gila River and Albert Ray and Wallace Anton of the Salt River Reservation. Their remains lie in foreign soil, and to these brave patriots we owe eternal gratitude.

Wallace, who appears in the photograph of Ross' company, was killed in the great Argonne Forest drive just two days before the armistice was signed. Some of his friends have reported his observation when he saw the front line: *"Pegih neh! Ai att heg t-gahgi!* (Well, we have reached what we have been after!)"

When I received the news of Wallace's death I was deeply grieved, for he had been my good friend and classmate at the Phoenix Indian School. He was a clean-cut chap, full of fun, and a bright student. And he was only one of the many Indians who died in World War I!

How unfair it seemed to me when the brave Indian volunteers returned home, still aliens in their native land. It was not until 1924 that Congress finally bestowed citizenship on us Indians. Oh, the irony of it!

*   *   *

In the spring of 1919, while I was taking exams for my junior year in high school, my dream of three years came true. Ross finally came back to Phoenix, his military service completed with honor. After a seven-year romance, at last we could be married. Of course we considered the possibility of a high school education for Ross, but this no longer seemed realistic. The returned soldier was now twenty-seven and as anxious as me to start a family. His three years of serving his country had brought an end to his educational hopes.

Ross had been trained as a tinner and plumber at the Indian School, and he found employment in these trades in a small shop. We rented a tiny house near his work and my high school and settled there together, legally married in the traditional Indian fashion. As my senior year progressed, however, we decided that we should also be wed in the white man's way. I would soon have a diploma — why not a marriage certificate?

Thus the year 1920 was a big one for Ross and me. First came my graduation, which made Ross so very proud. I have to admit that I also felt a certain pride when one of the commencement speakers pointed out that our class was unique in so far as it included the first full-blood Pima Indian girl graduate. None of my dear ones were there to hear that speech — Ross was working nights, and transportation and money problems prevented my parents from coming. My brother Bill was in Chicago, attending a school of music and scrimping to live at the YMCA. But although I missed my family, it was impossible for me to feel lonely, for I was surrounded by proud friends and employees from the Indian School. The Heflins, the family with whom I had recently lived, were also there, wishing me well and giving me gifts.

Our simple wedding, which followed soon after graduation, was also attended by just a few. The ceremony took place in Dr. Clarence Ellis' manse at Salt River. Ross' sister Jennie and one of Dr. Ellis' missionary friends were the witnesses. We had very few gifts and no reception: in those hard postwar times we simply could not afford the old Pima custom of *hemapig* (gathering), with all the traditional hospitality and feasting.

It did seem only right though, to try to honor another old Pima tradition — that of living with Ross' parents for a short time at least. After all, I hardly knew my new family, and they had had little chance to become acquainted with me. Ross would have to limit his visiting to the weekends because of his job in Phoenix, but at least I could take this chance to get to know my parents-in-law.

The Shaws lived in an old-fashioned Pima home made of saguaro ribs caulked with mud. Indoors, stout mesquite posts held up the log ceilings. There was no plumbing, gas, or electricity. How difficult this simple way of life seemed to Ross and me after our years of enjoying the white man's conveniences!

Ross' mother labored with such sweet patience. How could I help but do the work she expected of me as a new daughter-in-law? Every morning at 3:00 A.M. I would rise to put on the beans and make a huge stack of tortillas for breakfast. Then at 5:00 Mother Shaw would awaken the boys with her traditional call: "You never rest until you die!"

After breakfast Ross' father and brothers would trudge out to their little forty-acre farm, where they walked behind their horse-drawn plow and sowed seeds of cotton, wheat, corn, and beans. After only a short afternoon break they would return to the fields to labor until sundown.

Despite such hard work, the Shaws were always poor,

Ross' parents lived in an old-fashioned house like this one, built of saguaro ribs caulked with mud. The log ceilings and brush roof were supported by mesquite posts. This sort of house, along with the adobe, replaced the olas kih of my childhood. Today many modern Pimas live in fine concrete block houses, such as those in the pictures near the end of this book.

barely able to buy a few groceries each month. Our hearts ached for them in their difficult existence, but both Ross and I knew that laboring beside his parents in the fields each day was not the best way to help. The educations they had strived so hard to give us had prepared us to bring in money from the white man's world; it would be wrong to waste all those years of schooling on a life of primitive farming.

So after only one month of living with the Shaws we left, filled with mixed emotions. True, we had been educated in the white man's ways, but we were still traditional Pimas with strong feelings of duty to our families and an intense love of our land. Perhaps in our hearts we would always be farmers.

Even with the knowledge that we would return on weekends to help with the work and send money for groceries regularly, we felt pangs of guilt and loss as we packed up our meager belongings and set out to try to make a life of our own in the city of Phoenix.

A Unit in the Family of America

ROSS AND I BEGAN our life in Phoenix during times of unemployment and economic deprivation. It was a blessing that he had a good-paying job, and we knew it.

Just before our little wedding, Ross had lost his position in the tin shop, for the owner had been forced to close his business and let his workers go. It was fortunate that a relative told my husband of a vacancy at the railroad depot. The American Railway Express Company, then known as Wells Fargo, employed a number of Indian boys.

Ross started at the bottom, loading trains on the graveyard shift. However, James M. Williams, the general agent, told him that in this company anyone could climb the ladder as high as he desired, and Ross took his challenging advice to heart.

As long as he lived, Mr. Williams helped to make sure that in truth discrimination did not exist at ARE (now REA). Sometimes an Indian employee drank firewater, and found himself incarcerated in the city jail. Mr. Williams would bail him out, collect for him on payday, and help him to return to work. The boys were all grateful for such kind concern, and all of them mourned their boss' passing. His son Jack, who used to play barefoot around the depot, became governor of the state of Arizona, a tribute to the guidance of his wise and generous father.

Mr. Williams never just mouthed nice-sounding sayings. He meant what he said, and he saw to it that his words were carried out in action. The truth of his statement about unlimited advancement for minority people was proved by the career of Ross. When the ARE office posted a notice of a vacancy for a driver, Ross, a humble loader of trains, applied and was accepted.

In those days Phoenix was a small town of unpaved streets, and horse-drawn vehicles were as common as motor cars. Ross delivered packages to the residential area north of town in a wagon drawn by workhorses. Sometimes the team was unmanageable, especially when there was unusual excitement, such as a parade, in the streets of Phoenix.

In addition to driving the wagon, it was Ross' duty to load and unload the goods it held. Sometimes dogs and cats objected to being crated, and Ross would have to give them a merry chase to get them boxed up for their owners. The trunks he carried were as heavy as lead, but he was young and strong, and he never dropped one. His customers appreciated the assistance he gave them, and this helped ease the prejudice against Indians which was so prevalent in those early days.

After several years of driving the delivery wagon, Ross was promoted to the position of receiving clerk. His work now required weighing packages and figuring the cost of shipments. This, of course, involved working with the public, and every once in a while Ross again would encounter the prejudice that hurts minority people so. Sometimes a customer would actually insist that a white man wait on him. But the company would not put up with such insults to its employees, and such people were always sent back to Ross' counter. In the end, their prejudice only succeeded in losing them considerable time. Who knows at what point in their lives they were so misguided as to believe that all Indians are bad at figures!

Sometimes Ross would tell me stories of how he had encountered similar attitudes when he was defending his country in the war. I often marveled at his patience and reserved for him the old Pima expression — "a man of iron nerves."

Luckily, Ross' fellow employees at American Railway Express were far from prejudiced. Roscoe, as he was familiarly known around the office, in a few years was promoted to a position of great trust — that of money clerk. In a little cubbyhole office which he shared with a big safe, he kept accurate accounts of all valuable goods which had been shipped. He was the only one on his shift permitted to go into this room, where all large packages were locked. He was also the only one who knew the combination to the big safe and a smaller one in the baggage car room, where highly valuable packages and moneybags were kept. Two other men had these responsibilities on other shifts, and each carried a small pistol on his belt at all times as protection against thieves.

Ross enjoyed the position of money clerk and the duties it entailed. The job was never dull, and nearly every day he would come home with a tale of excitement or humor. As the years went on, he took on the job of foreman, routing freight to the proper drivers. In the end he left with sad as well as happy feelings, he so much enjoyed his job and the people he worked with.

*   *   *

That anyone could be prejudiced against Ross seemed strange to me, for I found no such attitudes in the multi-racial neighborhood we lived in. While Ross was working at American Railway Express, I was busy making a home of the small house we had rented. The place was located in a crowded, happy neighborhood which housed many Mexican-Americans as well as Indians and whites of a number of national origins. I enjoyed learning how other people lived and how their traditional foods were prepared.

Once our home was established, I had little time to relax. Our son Roderick Ross was born within a few months, and he was soon followed by a little girl, whom we named Adeline Ethel. Like most Indian women of the time, I was much too modest to have my babies delivered by a doctor in a hospital. Instead I returned to the reservation and gave birth in Ross' parents' saguaro-rib home, attended by his paternal grandmother Yellow Flowers and my mother Rose Moore.

Now that we had children, we were especially glad for our friendly Phoenix neighbors. Little Roddy and Addy were able to substitute neighborhood pals for the many uncles and aunts and cousins Ross and I had enjoyed during our reservation childhoods.

*   *   *

Twice in their early lives, however, our toddlers were able to meet their Uncle Bill, who visited us from Chicago whenever he had the time and money. By now Bill had

I am holding our eighteen-month-old son, while our seven-month-old baby girl sits in the carriage. Back then I thought, "Oh my goodness! I'll probably have so many children, and all so close together!" As it happened, the Lord blessed us with only three — Roddy, Addy, and much later little Billy.

graduated from music school. His Indian School trade training served him well, for he was able to find a job as a cabinet-maker with the Illinois Bell Telephone Company. In addition, he gave music lessons nights and weekends and played in musical groups whenever he had the time.

Bill no longer lived in the YMCA but was now boarding with the famous Dr. Carlos Montezuma and his wife Mary in their stylish apartment on Michigan Avenue. It was through Bill's connection with this remarkable couple that we had the opportunity to host the great doctor in our humble home on Adams Street during his final illness.

The full story of this outstanding Indian is told in the Epilogue of this book. Suffice it to say here that he had risen through his own determination from a five-year-old Apache captive of the Pimas to one of America's highly respected surgeons. At the height of his career, when he was happily married to a lovely young German girl and blessed with many friends, he was stricken with diabetes, then an incurable disease. His Masonic brothers urged him to return to Arizona, where the mild climate might prolong his life. Although he longed to remain in Chicago, the center of his most precious memories, he finally decided to heed their advice. "Stay and store our furniture," he told his wife Mary. "Then you may follow me to Arizona."

So it was that in December 1922 a yellow paper called a telegram was received at 1314 East Adams Street, Phoenix, Arizona. The message read: "Please meet Dr. Carlos Montezuma at the railroad station on Tuesday at 9:00 P.M. Left Chicago a very sick man. Your brother, Bill Moore."

Ross had just arrived home from work when the wire came. Montezuma the famous surgeon was going to visit us! We had both heard so much about him since the time when we were children on the reservation. Now we were going to meet him in our home!

But after the initial excitement, doubts and worries began to creep into our talk. Would our two active youngsters prove too noisy for the sick gentleman? How would we transport him from the station without a car? It occurred to us that we could borrow the auto which belonged to our Pima neighbors, but immediately we both agreed that this was out of the question. We remembered the values which had been stamped into our hearts by our traditional Indian parents: "Never borrow. Work hard to get what you need. Borrowed things never last."

So at eight o'clock Ross boarded the trolley bound for the railroad station. As the train pulled to a stop, he wondered how he would recognize the famous passenger. Then he saw a distinguished Indian sitting in a Pullman car, and he knew that this was the man he was looking for.

Ross politely introduced himself and asked, "Are you Dr. Montezuma?" "Yes, yes, I am," said the older man. "But where are my Apache relatives, the Dickens family, who were supposed to meet me and take me to the reservation?" Ross knew nothing of this arrangement, but he told Montezuma about Bill's telegram while he and a porter helped the sick man to a taxicab.

In the meantime, I sat at home with butterflies in my tummy. Luckily Roddy and Addy were sleeping soundly, so I quieted my nerves by preparing a light snack in case our guest proved hungry. My heart jumped when I heard footsteps on the porch. I was a young and inexperienced hostess. Would I be able to care for the doctor in a way he would find acceptable?

Ross introduced our guest and led him into the living room. The initial awkwardness I felt was soon over, for the great man kept repeating, "You so much resemble your brother Bill. He is a fine boy. My Billy, my Billy!" As tears flowed down his face, my heart went out to him. The butterflies in my stomach flew out the window; it seemed as though we had known each other all our lives. The famous Indian surgeon was indeed a kind and humble man.

*   *   *

I awoke before dawn, as I did every morning, to send Ross off to his job. Our children were up early, curious about the visitor in our house. When Montezuma arose he treated them with special kindness. "Give them fruit, cookies, and gum from my lunch basket," he told me. I gave the toddlers the goodies and hurriedly herded them outdoors before they forgot their manners.

But sometimes we parents do not give our children credit, and we often underestimate their good common sense. Roddy and Addy were little angels during those five days Dr. Montezuma stayed in our home, waiting for his Apache relatives to take him to Fort McDowell. They played outdoors all day in the fenced yard, coming in only occasionally for cookies or a drink of water. After lunch, they obediently went to take their naps. I was free to devote all my time to the sick man.

Every day it was the same routine. Dr. Montezuma would eat and nap and wonder why his relatives had not

During the five days that we were privileged to care for the great Dr. Carlos Montezuma, his fighting words changed our lives. In those times of prejudice, he made us realize that the Indian is not inferior, but a person of great dignity and worth. We set out to prove this to the world.

come for him yet. Modern medicine had been able to do nothing for his illness, and he thought that the Apache medicine man might be able to cure him.

Sometimes, when he was feeling good, Dr. Montezuma would sit with me and talk about the subject uppermost in his mind — the struggle for freedom for the American Indian. For years he had been giving speeches which urged the Indian to tolerate the white man's prejudice no longer. Now I was hearing those stirring phrases right in the living room of my home!

How well I remember some of those words! Later I procured a copy of the address Montezuma made before the Society of American Indians in Lawrence, Kansas, in 1915. Some of the lines from that speech still inspire me today:

"Patient, silent, and distant the Indian race has been these many years. But there comes a time in human events when abandonment of racial responsibilities becomes very oppressive, unbearable, intolerable . . . then man must exert himself, speak, and act. Our heritage is freedom, but we are not free. Wake up, Indians, all over America! We stand helpless, innocently waiting for the fulfillment of promises that will never be fulfilled. . . .

" . . . As a race, we are at a crisis. Our position as a race and our rights must not be questioned. Looking from all points of the compass, there is only one object for this society of Indians to work for, namely, 'Freedom for our people!'

"There is a wrong feeling, a wrong thought, and a wrong judgment that we must fight. It is an individual battle! It is called prejudice. To tackle prejudice, it is better to do it face to face in the busy world. To play the same card as the other fellow, we must know him.

"To fight is to forget ourselves as Indians in the world. To think of one's self as different from the mass is unhealthy. Push forward as one of them, be congenial and be in harmony with your environment and make yourselves feel at home as one of the units in the big family of America. Make good, deliver the goods and convince the world by your character that the Indians are not as they have been misrepresented to be."

The reader can imagine how such thoughts helped Ross and me back in 1922, when we were young and struggling to make a life for ourselves in the white man's city. These ideas gave Ross the courage to ignore the prejudice he encountered from the public at his job, and later they helped us to move into an all-white, "restricted" neighborhood.

It was with deep sadness that we watched our guest depart with the Dickens couple in their open Ford automobile. I cringed when I thought of the road the frail man would have to travel. It was rough and narrow, full of ruts and bumps, over a stretch of wild desert populated only by cacti, sagebrush, and coyotes. Scottsdale was then a one-horse town with only a few houses and farms. What if the doctor should become seriously ill on the way?

That night Ross and I sat at the kitchen table, talking of our guest. We missed him terribly. Although he had been with us only five days, we had become deeply attached to him and his inspiring words. Only a Pima expression can describe the loss we felt — *hahawanimath*. Full interpretation of this phrase is impossible, but the literal meaning is "The ravens overwhelmed us." It is used when someone leaves your home after you have become accustomed to him; you have a feeling of emptiness, sadness, and longing.

When I went to clean Dr. Montezuma's room and air his bedding in the sun before laundering it, I was surprised to find five silver dollars on the night table near the bed. Of course we did not expect any pay, but this was our guest's way of showing his gratefulness for his stay. It was his expression of the old Indian tradition of paying for services rendered as well as a reminder that Indian people are generous by nature.

When I showed the money to Ross he said, "The white man says we Indians are not a competitive race. Well, I guess they are right, and I am glad of it! The Indian would rather share with his fellow man than to horde money and worldly goods. We cannot take it with us when death calls." Ross had been so inspired by the fighting words of Dr. Carlos Montezuma that he was starting to sound like him!

In the latter part of December, Mrs. Montezuma arrived at our home. No sooner had she sat down than she received a telegram: "Your husband is very low. Please come at once." We believed the message was from Dr. Clarence Ellis, our missionary at Salt River, who had been making regular visits to Dr. Montezuma. Later we heard the telegram had been sent by Dr. Stroud of Tempe, a temporary government doctor.

Mary Montezuma was driven to the reservation, where she found her husband in a weak condition, lying on the dirt floor of an Apache wickiup. She moved him to a little frame house nearby and cared for him until he went to his rest on January 23, 1923. The medicine men had been powerless to heal the diabetic man.

Ross had to work, but my sister-in-law Jennie and I had the privilege of attending Montezuma's funeral at the First Baptist Church in Phoenix. The pallbearers, chosen from the students at the Phoenix Indian School, included two Pimas, William Sampson and Juan V. Adams, and Timothy Ethelbah, an Apache. Later the boys' dorm at the school was given Dr. Montezuma's Apache name — *Wasaja* (Beckoning or Signaling).

Before he died, the great humanitarian had requested that he be buried on top of Superstition Peak, but it was impossible to fulfill this wish. Instead he was placed in the Fort McDowell cemetery, where a beautiful monument marks his grave. Before the burial another funeral service was held in the Presbyterian church at Fort McDowell. It was attended by members of the doctor's Yavapai Apache tribe and led by men of the Masonic Order, of which the deceased had been a staunch member.

After the burial, Mrs. Montezuma, whom we soon were calling Mary, came to stay at our home for several months in order to avoid returning to Chicago in the winter. We enjoyed every aspect of her stay with our family, but we were especially interested in her reminiscences of her famous husband, whom we had been privileged to care for during his last sickness. The biography of Dr. Montezuma which appears in the Epilogue of this book has been based on these conversations with his widow after his death.

Interestingly, it was a true act of Providence that Mary Montezuma chose to honor our particular family with her extended visit. As we formed a close friendship, little did either of us suspect that we would soon become sisters-in-law! In 1924 we received the happy news that Mary had married my brother Bill. They purchased a fine home in Blue Island, Illinois, and took in J. Newton's two little boys, Everett and Russell Moore, as their own. What a joy it was for us to know that our friend Mary had found happiness once again! The story of their warm and music-filled household is told by my nephew Everett in the Epilogue of this book.

*   *   *

Our little house on Adams Street was also filled with warmth and happiness. We forever will cherish our memories of the events that occurred there — the early childhood days of Roddy and Addy and the visits of the great Carlos Montezuma and his wife. But memories don't make up for inconvenience, and now that it seemed likely that Ross would make his career at ARE we wanted to be within walking distance of the depot.

So it was that in 1924 we decided to move to a pleasant home on West Grant Street. Besides our friends the Mexican-Americans, this neighborhood housed a number of black people, many of whom we came to know well. The words of Dr. Montezuma often came to our minds here: "Make yourselves feel at home as one of the units in the big family of America." This command was really put into action in this little section of Phoenix, where persons of every race lived together as one big happy family.

I was glad that Roddy and Addy had the privilege of growing up in this nonprejudiced atmosphere. Their little Mexican-American friends taught them Spanish, which they could speak fluently before they had learned their own Pima tongue. These charming children also helped my little ones to have good manners, for their parents had trained them well. Whenever they were called, they always answered, "Yes, ma'am" or "Si, señora," and immediately ran home to find out what they needed to do.

The Garcías lived next door to us, and their children became our little ones' special friends. Besides the Spanish language, Roddy and Addy learned many Mexican customs and superstitions. I particularly remember one time when little Patrick remarked, "Roddy and sister, please step on my new shoes."

"Why should we step on your shoes?" asked my curious son.

"So you will bring good luck, and the shoes will last longer," replied Pat. After that, our children took up the custom and always made sure to step on each other's new shoes.

Patrick García was just one year older than our son, and the two of them were classmates until they were ready for Phoenix Union High School, which Pat could not attend due to a lack of funds. He was a brilliant boy, and we have always regretted that he had to miss that part of his education. Rod and Pat remain good friends today, and when they get together they still converse in the Spanish language.

Our black next-door neighbors were also very fine people. They had no children and worked at the Phoenix Country Club all day. Their ferocious-looking part-bull-dog named Jimmie was left lonely for attention, and he got plenty from our family. Jimmie's looks were deceiving, for he was good-humored, tolerant of the children's attentions, and always ready for a romp. Every day he would park himself on our porch and function as a sort of dog-babysitter. When I would scold the children for playing in the street, Jimmie would run to me and growl as if to say, "What's the matter — don't you trust me? *I'm* looking out for them!" In the end, Jimmie spent so much time at our house that his owners decided to give him to us. We were overjoyed to take him as our pet, but we realized what a great sacrifice it must have been for our friends to give up such a good dog.

Another fine black family on the street was named Jackson. Mrs. Jackson was a widow who had to pick cotton to make ends meet. While she was working, her many little ones would come over to play with Roddy and Addy in our yard. In later years we heard that one of the Jackson girls had married Leon Thompson, a Phoenix policeman of great integrity, who endeared himself to all classes of people. It once again proved to us that minority people *can* climb the ladder of success by hard work.

Throughout our lives this conviction, so eloquently preached by Dr. Carlos Montezuma, was proved out again and again. It was the philosophy we tried to instill in our children as they grew up in the white man's world, still encountering occasional examples of racial prejudice. At such times we would remind them of the words of the great Indian doctor: "To fight is to forget ourselves as Indians in the world. To think of one's self as different from the mass is unhealthy. Make good, deliver the goods, and convince the world by your character that the Indians are not as they have been misrepresented to be." Rod and Adeline, today completely at home in the big family of America, bear out the value of this teaching.

The Passing of the Old

IN 1930 WE MOVED our little family to a newer home on nearby West Sherman Street. Once again we enjoyed making friendships with people of all backgrounds and races.

These were very happy days for us. Besides the sounds of laughter and talking in two languages, our home was filled with the strains of music.

Neither Ross nor I had learned to play a musical instrument, and we were determined that our children would receive a solid musical training. The lessons were expensive, but we denied ourselves many pleasures to make them possible. Roddy took up the violin, while Addy chose the piano.

Of course we had help from my brother Bill, who by now had a number of devoted music students and had organized several drum and bugle corps. In addition, he played solo cornet for the Chicago Board of Trade and performed violin and cornet solos for many other organizations. Bill sent Roddy a violin and helped pay for his lessons. By giving up luxuries, we managed to find money for a used piano for Addy.

In the end it was all worth the many sacrifices, for our youngsters came to love good classical music. But how often we regretted the fact that Ross did not take advantage of the wonderful opportunity to learn music at the Tucson Mission School! Convinced that piano-playing was a sissy thing, he had hidden under the porch of the Girls' Building instead of going to his music lessons. What we would have given for those free lessons now!

Besides the recreation that music provided, we had baseball for more rousing fun. Radio and television had not yet been invented, and the few movie theaters showed only silent films with long, hard-to-read title cards. You can see why a lively ball game was always a welcome way to relax and let off steam.

We Shaws were especially enthusiastic about the sport because Ross was one of the American Railway Express Company's star players. He was catcher, while Walter Webb, a Quechan Indian from the Colorado River Reservation, was the outstanding pitcher. Both men were straight as the arrows of their ancestors and strong as the Spartans of Greece. Indeed, Webb could have been another Jim Thorpe and played professional ball if he had so desired.

Every Sunday during the baseball season games were played in the city's many parks. Various local companies sponsored teams, and sometimes the competition got quite hot. ARE's two Indian players proved to be a big drawing card for the team; wherever they played a large crowd of fans followed to cheer them on to victory.

Once an amusing incident took place at Eastlake Park, so named because of a beautiful manmade lake adjoining the athletic field. An important game was at its climax, with the ARE boys in the outfield. The fans were hoarse from rooting, and the warm air was charged with heated arguments.

The teams were working hard and soaked with sweat. Webb, the pitcher, was the only player who remained calm and cool. He smiled his unusual smile, like a cat ready to pounce on a helpless mouse, as he cautiously glanced around, ready at a moment's notice to catch the runner trying to steal second base. With assurance he hurled the ball to Ross, who squatted close to the ground, arms stretched forth to receive it.

Suddenly the crowd screamed! The bat cracked against the ball, and a fly went soaring toward the fielder, Art Lowry. Art backed up swiftly, his eyes on the small dot in the air. As it plunged toward him, he stretched out his arms, ready for the impact of a sure catch. No one can describe the comical shock on Art's face as he unwittingly backed himself into the lake, ducking himself along with the ducks! The crowd roared with cheers and laughter, the tense moment broken.

What a predicament! With a sheepish grin, Art returned to his position on the field, his baseball suit dripping. His loyalty and fine sportsmanship helped us to win the game that day.

*   *   *

Looking back on our happy family life, our story seems so simple. Yet I have already taken pages and pages to tell about it. Perhaps the Pimas who read this book will say I am like Ban, the coyote — boastful and over-talkative about myself. No traditional Pima would ever talk long about himself for fear this charge would be thrown up to him. In any case, it is surely time to return to the reservation for a while to catch up on the lives of my parents, Josiah and Rose Moore, formerly known as Red Arrow and Haus Molly.

I have told so much of our city life that it must seem to the reader that we no longer missed the old ways and our many friends and relatives who still farmed along the Gila and Salt rivers. This is not so. Throughout our more than forty years in Phoenix we always planned a retirement on the reservation, and our every vacation and many weekends were spent there. The little reservation youngsters often reciprocated with visits to their city cousins, who delightedly would show them the wonders of urban life.

Ross was always so kind and generous. He understood how hard it was for the old people, tilling out a meager living on the rocky soil, now without the abundant water supply their ancestors had known. The white man had depleted the ever-flowing Gila for his own projects, and in many places the once-fertile Pima farms were now dry and barren.

When water became scarce at Gila Crossing, Josiah often thought of the fertile fields at Sacate, the place of his birth. Visions of fat watermelons and rows of tall corn haunted him. Finally, when we children were all grown, the bold old man moved back to Sacate. Here he cleared new fields and was proud of his good yields, but the farm work grew harder for him as the years passed by.

From the time we were married Ross had tried to help out, buying groceries for my parents one week and for his parents the next. Whenever we could we visited the reservations to help with the heavier chores.

Ross' mom and dad were lucky; besides Ross they had several sons who lived near them to lend a helping hand. My parents, however, of all their eleven children, by now had only me and my sister Lillie to offer them aid and comfort; Bill lived too far away to see them often.

Lillie had married a Maricopa and gone to live in an adobe house at Lehi. She was very traditional in her living style, but she had a brilliant mind, which enabled her to pick up English from her children and grandchildren. She could also quickly learn to use the white man's conveniences, such as a treadle sewing machine and a clock. Ross used to love her thick bread, and every time we went to visit her she would bake enough for us to take plenty home.

My older brother J. Newton had labored so hard to make a better life for his children. We all felt that it was overwork that finally caused him to contract tuberculosis in the early 1920s. This was when we still lived on Adams Street, and once when Bill came to visit from Chicago he persuaded our brother to go to the Indian TB hospital in Phoenix. Newton died soon after that, but he had achieved what he had wanted so badly all along — a better way of life for his children. All of them spoke English and held responsible jobs in the white man's world.

These children of Newton's, along with those of Lillie, felt a strong obligation to help their aged grandparents. They visited them and offered aid whenever they could. In addition, from the time they were six and seven years old, Addy and Roddy spent their Christmas vacations helping the old folks on their reservation farm. When we picked the children up in our little Ford car, we were always pleased to hear how much of the Pima language they had learned.

Their grandparents also told them the ancient legends and fed them the traditional Pima foods. But although they were too polite to complain much, our children really didn't care for the old ways. They were far more at home in the world of the white man, and they preferred hot dogs and fried chicken to succotash and pinole.

It was easy for us to see that the old traditions would soon be lost. The reality of the "generation gap" is shown by the following story. Once one of J. Newton's girls bought a postcard in a drugstore to send to her grand-father, Josiah Moore. Its photo, which is reproduced on p. 68 of this book, was captioned, "Maricopa Indian and his second wife." When he received the picture, Josiah was surprised to see that the man in the photograph was his father-in-law. Evidently the photographer had assumed that Black Shirt was a Maricopa because he spoke the language so fluently. "Little did my granddaughter know," laughed Josiah, "that she was buying a picture of her very own great-grandfather!"

*   *   *

As I saw the old beliefs of my people slipping away, my heart felt deep sadness. It was during those years that I resolved that I would someday do all that I could to pre-serve what was left of my people's traditions. I began to closely watch all that remained of the ancient lore and customs. Soon it would be too late, for the old ones were fast departing from this earth, taking their songs and festivals with them.

The reader can imagine the thrill I felt when on one of

our visits to Salt River I learned that the older inhabitants were planning to once again celebrate the ancient festival of Ho'ok Mehitha. This was my people's dramatization of the old story of the burning of the witch that Grandmother Song Endings had repeated to us children so long ago.

The missionaries' belief that the traditional customs were sinful was gradually dying out. Now that the Pimas were staunch Christians, it seemed better to allow an occasional celebration, so that the ancient dream-songs given to the Indians through visions sent by their *jijosh* (gods) would not be lost forever.

On the day of the Witch-Burning festival, large groups of Pimas flocked to the dance grounds in wagons, on horseback, and on foot. There was a savory feast of beef barbecue, chili stew, and tortillas, topped off with home-grown watermelons. Afterwards Indians of all ages played baseball, competed in a rodeo, and participated in foot and potato sack races.

"Why, this is just like the white man's Fourth of July!" I whispered to Ross. "When will they come to the Burning of the Witch?" Finally, as the sun went down, the event I had come to see commenced. The old ones sang the since-forgotten Ho'ok Mehitha song. Then the singers beat on cardboard boxes in place of woven baskets, long into the night, to their hearts' content. The men chose partners and danced in full swing. When the Going Home song was heard, the people began to gather up their children and belongings. "My songs are over. Return to your homes, taking my beautiful songs," chanted the singers.

As Ross and I watched the Pimas leaving the rosy firelit circle, moving off into the clear white moonlight, we could almost imagine that it was the time before the white man, when a celebration such as this one was the only break from the constant tilling of the soil. We were glad that our lives now held so much more, but in our hearts we could not help but feel sadness for the ancient beliefs that were passing away.

*   *   *

Watching the Ho'ok Mehitha celebration must have been even more emotional for Red Arrow and Haus Molly, our dear Josiah and Rose Moore. They had lived many years and seen many changes wrought by the white-complexioned people with a language too difficult for them to learn.

Now the day had come when Red Arrow was too old and infirm to work his land. After a long talk, Ross and I paid the old ones a visit one evening in 1929.

"We know it will be hard, father and mother," I said, "but we want you to come to live with us in Phoenix. Only there can we give you the care you deserve."

The bravery and strength of these two old people was shown again as they pulled up their deep roots at their Sacate home and climbed into our little Ford one Saturday afternoon. The city of Phoenix was a new and foreign environment to them, but they were able to adjust and live in contentment. Their grandchildren helped brighten their days and even taught them some English words.

My mother still wove her fine Pima baskets from supplies she had brought from the reservation. Although she was in her eighties, her eyesight was still good, and her baskets were among the most beautiful I had ever seen.

Grandfather Josiah was still bold enough to occasionally take in an entirely new adventure, such as a motion picture show. Once after he and eight-year-old Roddy had gone to see a film, our son told a funny story at the dinner table. "When grandpa saw a man pushed into a lake on the screen, he hollered out, *'Haia o'othham!* [poor fellow!]' All the people stared; I guess they didn't know Pima." Red Arrow's old eyes twinkled as Roddy spoke, and at family reunions thereafter we always told that story and laughed.

When they had lived with us for almost four years, our aged parents made yet another change. My brother Bill came and took them to his home in Blue Island. Again they adjusted to their new surroundings, although mother was failing fast. She still did her weaving, but now she spent more and more time in bed. Finally in April 1934 I received a wire asking me to come to Chicago at once.

Bill met eleven-year-old Addy and me at the train. He took my hand and said, "The doctor tells us her age is against her — her heart is like worn-out machinery. The end is only a matter of time."

We were relieved to see that mother was still conscious. When she saw Addy and me she cried. We all cried. Within two weeks she had left us. Her remains were brought back to Arizona, where she was buried beside her loved ones. Josiah returned with us.

Father was left alone to bear his grief, but his faith in God was his great comfort. He also found solace in an old friend to whom he could talk in his waning days. By this time Ross' mother had also passed away, and his father Jacob was anxious for company. On our frequent visits to the Salt River Reservation the two oldtimers would sit in the sun for hours, recalling the days of their youths.

Ross' father never knew that I was expecting another baby. In those days we were too modest to talk of such things. Now my heart bleeds when I think of how this proud old gentleman would have been thrilled to know he would soon have another grandchild. He passed away just months before the baby was born in 1937.

Because I was now over forty and the doctors foresaw the possibility of complications, I had my last child in the Phoenix Indian Hospital. How different it was from the rough mud house in which I had chosen to have Rod and Addy!

Although Ross' father missed seeing his new grandson, little William Newton was able to bring the sunniness of childhood into Red Arrow's last years. The old one delighted in seeing the infant learn to sit, then crawl, and finally toddle about on two chubby legs. Every morning Billy would run into my father's room to shake hands, repeating, "baba," his word for grandpa, over and over again.

*   *   *

One night in 1939 I was awakened by father's coughing. I jumped up from bed and hurried to his room. When I turned on the light, I found him very sick, his face unusually pale. "My maghm, are you feeling ill?" I asked him anxiously.

"Yes, daughter Anna, my time is here. I have prayed for this time, to be taken home to my Lord. Anna, feel my feet — are they cold?" I felt his feet and answered yes.

"Are my eyes glassy?"

"Yes, my dear father."

"These are the signs to go by." The brave old man sighed and settled back on his pillows.

"Father, should I call our neighbors to come?"

"No, no, let's not bother their sleep. Just you and I will go through this night, waiting out my time. But do you think it would be possible for my Bill to come from Chicago while I am still alive?"

"We will call him," I promised. "And we will also bring Lillie from Lehi."

In the morning father was still conscious and waiting for my sister. When Ross returned from his night shift at the depot, he drove at once to bring her. She was with us when the end came at 3:00 P.M. We tried to hold back our tears as father gave us his last message:

"I have lived a long time now. I am ready to go to meet my God. I have made all my plans about the land I own. It will last you and your descendants a long time. Do not ever sell it, my children."

With those words Red Arrow quietly passed away, at peace with himself and his God at the ripe age of ninety-one. We sent a quick wire to my brother Bill, who came at once to take charge of the funeral arrangements and most of the expenses.

After father's remains had been taken to the mortuary, little Billy ran into the old man's room and stood by the empty bed. "Where baba?" he repeated over and over again. We tried to help him understand that his baba had gone to heaven. But how does one explain death to a two-year-old child?

The Power of Music

MY FATHER RED ARROW was the last of our parents to leave this earth. Pimas feel a strong obligation to their elders, and it had been our comfort and privilege to help our old ones in their waning years. But this privilege had not been without its financial burdens; only now that our parents were gone could we begin to consider the possibility of buying a home of our own.

The decision brought about long discussions around the kitchen table. At first Ross was against the idea of another house in Phoenix. "Why should we buy a home here?" he asked. "I have my own land, inherited from my father, where we can build a house. Perhaps the time has come for us to go back to farming on the reservation. I don't want to live among the white people all the rest of my life."

I understood how my husband felt. His company had recently passed a retirement plan, and social security had finally been enacted by the U.S. government. This meant that we could go back to farming with a little assured income to keep us in our old age. But the time didn't seem quite right to me yet.

"Ross, you are forgetting one important thing," I said, pointing to little Billy, who was playing with pots and pans on the kitchen floor. "If we go back to the reservation now, what will we do about the education of our children? Rod will graduate from high school this year, but he wants to go on to college. How can we afford it if he can't live at home?

"And what about Adeline? She is only a sophomore now — where would she finish high school? Surely you don't want to put her in a BIA boarding school!

"As for Billy — he has his whole education in front of him. Do you want him to go to the BIA schools and learn only a manual trade, as we did? Certainly we owe him a good education in the white man's culture, with the opportunity to go on to college if he wants."

Ross looked defeated. In his heart he knew I was right; his dream of returning to the reservation would have to be postponed. Later, as he looked back on his life, he felt glad that we stayed in Phoenix at that time. "God must have been with us, Anna," he has often told me. "All my life God has been helping me, and everything is coming the way I want it to happen."

*   *   *

Those were the hard years marked by the beginning of World War II and the tail end of the Great Depression. Many were walking the streets, looking for any kind of a job. We were fortunate in that Ross had employment with ARE; the railroad would have to stop running before he joined the job-seekers.

We were also lucky to have accrued a bit of capital — enough to buy furniture and put a down payment on a home. Most of the articles in the stores, including the furniture we had waited so long to buy, were now selling at greatly reduced prices. Many people had lost their nice homes due to foreclosed mortgages, and in the glutted house market the costs were also down. Because of these reduced prices, we were able to buy better furniture and a much finer house than we otherwise could have afforded.

We requested a real estate agent to show us some homes in a neighborhood near a good school. We fell in love with a Spanish-type dwelling on West Jackson Street, only one block away from Jackson Elementary. It was surrounded by beautiful plantings and citrus trees, and the rooms were airy and spacious. What a thrill it would be to live in a house like this one! With elated spirits we awaited the acceptance of the contract. Finally the papers were ready, and we made the down payment.

But despite our excitement regarding our new house, we had certain misgivings about the neighborhood. In those days that part of the city was known as a "restricted area," where only white people lived. We wondered if our new neighbors would accept us, a family from "below the tracks" with copper Pima skins.

The real estate agent sensed our doubts and gave us reassurance. "Never mind," he said. "Just show them that you are good people, and their feelings of superiority will soon die out."

To our relief, most of our neighbors had no such feelings. But it only takes a few instances of snobbery to hurt a minority person. Right after we had moved to Jackson Street, a man in the meat market said loudly to the butcher, "I thought this was a restricted neighborhood." As he said the words, he glanced at me, to make sure I had heard.

I remembered the advice of the real estate agent and turned a deaf ear to the insult. When I told Ross about it that evening, he gave me good encouragement. "Imagine all the prejudice Dr. Montezuma must have come across during his career. But he rose above it and set up a medical practice that was open to people of all races. Prejudice will always be here, Anna. But if you want freedom for the Indian you must rise above the prejudice."

Ross' words brought to mind Montezuma's inspiring speeches. Then I thought of the many fine sermons I had heard glorifying the great eternal truths: "All are created by one Creator. All belong to the household of God." I resolved to ignore prejudice and set out to prove that the Indian is as good as any other nationality.

But it was hard to tell all this to a three-year-old. Little Billy just couldn't understand why the lady next door wouldn't let her small children play with him. I can still hear him crying on the porch, "Mama, let's go back to the old place!" He sorely missed his little Mexican-American friends.

*   *   *

Billy's spirits were lifted a bit by a visit from his Uncle Bill, Aunt Mary, and cousin Everett. We were so proud to show them around our new home, for the citrus trees were bearing luscious fruit, and the sun shone brightly into our many airy rooms filled with new furniture.

Bill was pleased for us, and, as always, he expressed his joy through music. He had a way of getting an orchestra together in short order, and soon he had persuaded the people across the street to join Rod with their violins.

My brother Bill Moore played a number of instruments in the drum and bugle corps he organized. Instead of pursuing fame for himself, he gave the gift of music to his many devoted students. Throughout his life Bill pursued excellence; he couldn't bear to do anything badly or even in an average way.

Others came to help, and our new home was soon filled with the strains of a beautiful classical concert. How happy I was that night, as I listened to my loved ones playing such wonderful music! A soft breeze blew through the windows, and my eyes filled with joyful tears.

The next day our violin-playing neighbors joined us on a happy picnic in the park. When we returned, our hair damp from swimming and our stomachs full of good food, my next-door neighbor said hello to me for the first time. She had heard the beautiful music the night before and wondered where it came from. I introduced her to Bill and Mary, and from then on the ice was broken. In no time our little ones had become close friends, running in and out of each other's houses for cookies and milk. The power of music had cut through this lady's barrier of prejudice.

*   *   *

We all hoped that racial prejudice was an attitude which was gradually dying out. Adeline almost never felt its stings in her classes and activities at Phoenix Union High School. Perhaps the younger generation was more enlightened in this regard than their elders.

When Rod entered Phoenix Junior College we thought he might find prejudice there, but during the course of his freshman year he never felt discrimination. He enjoyed his schooling so much that we all felt sad when he had to interrupt it to serve Uncle Sam.

At that time one year of military training was required of male citizens over twenty. "I think I should enlist," Rod told us. "It will only be for a year. I'll be home before you know it, back in college again." My son could tell that I was feeling disappointment and concern about the break in his education. Somehow I felt that it would be more than just a year, although I wasn't sure why.

As it turned out, my doubts were not without cause. On December 7, 1941, the Japanese bombed Pearl Harbor, involving our country in the fighting of World War II. Rod was in training at Fort Sill, Oklahoma, and we knew he would soon be called to active duty.

His first assignment was in Panama, where he was sent to guard the Canal Zone. After several months there he was selected to join a group of other noncommissioned officers at an officer candidate school at Fort Benning, Georgia. Here he grew impatient waiting for enrollment and volunteered for overseas service.

This was in October 1943. Sir Winston Churchill had just appealed to President Roosevelt for immediate help in destroying the strategic Japanese airfield at Myitkyina, Burma. A call went out for volunteers to go on a dangerous secret mission in this regard. What a coincidence! Rod and three of his courageous friends — Leroy Reeves, John Sutton, and Jack King — had just asked for immediate overseas service. They left for Burma before the month was out.

The secret nature of the assignment made it hard on all of us back home. Rod could not tell us where he was going, and his letters were always punctuated with pages cut by the censor's scissors. As nearly as we could figure, the boys had boarded an old ship and sailed around South America and the African Cape of Good Hope.

In Burma they joined a special outfit made up of hardy Guadalcanal veterans, under the sharp leadership of

"Vinegar" Joe Stillwell. They had no official designation as artillery, infantry, or cavalry, but they called themselves "Merrill's Marauders" to show their love for and faith in Frank Merrill. Secretly they used the label "Galahad." One war correspondent described them as the "nuttiest, goofiest, and lousiest young men of the U.S. to land in the China/India/Burma conflict."

It was certainly true that these boys knew how to laugh in the midst of peril. Once Rod wrote us that some of his Ozark buddies had shot and barbecued a wild turkey. When a British soldier saw them trussing the bird, he ran away hollering, "Them Yankees have killed a buzzard and are going to eat it!"

Despite such funny misunderstandings, the men all got on famously. Rod wrote us that Americans from all walks of life were living together in the steamy jungles like brothers with a common cause. Perhaps that was the key — every man wanted with all his heart to capture that strategic Japanese air base.

Rod proudly told us how the Japanese-Americans in his combat area fooled the Japanese by telling them, "The American troops went that way." Pleased by the apparent loyalty of their racial brothers, the Japanese unwittingly heeded their advice. Actually the Japanese-Americans had sent them on a wild goose chase, and as a result strategic points were demolished and American lives were saved.

Besides a single cause, Merrill's Marauders had another thing in common. All of them were bold and brave, afraid of nothing from the guardhouse to Hades. Once they climbed a six-thousand-foot mountain in the monsoon season with Japanese snipers shooting at them all the way to the summit. Rod said his hair was on end and his teeth were chattering as they scaled the steep walls. The mules, loaded down with ammunition, frequently slipped into gorges. Many of the men caught severe colds and were exhausted. But their toughness and bravery kept them from giving up.

When Rod told me about this adventure, I was reminded of the courage of his Great-granduncle Turtle, who once slid on his war shield into a canyon filled with Apaches. Turtle would surely have been proud of the determination and fearlessness of his modern-day descendant.

The hardships which Rod's unit had to undergo also reminded me of the old Pima war trails. For seventy-two days the boys lived in foxholes, dodging Japanese machine-gun fire. In the midst of the filth, disease, and discomfort that this existence entailed, they kept their sense of humor and never thought of giving up. The odds were overwhelming, but Merrill's Marauders stood their ground. In the words of Major General Stillwell, it was a "hellava fight."

In the end the men's persistence and bravery won them their goal. On September 4, 1943, they captured the muddy airfield at Myitkyina. No longer would Japanese planes take off from this base to drop deadly bombs on Allied targets.

But our son was not able to share in the elation of victory. He was wounded in that last decisive battle and immediately contracted typhus, a disease which had been a sure death in the days of World War I. Rod was carried to a hospital in India.

At home in Phoenix a telegram notified us of our beloved son's condition. It came around bedtime, and my husband and I wept like babies. Little Billy prayed for the safety of his "inclining brother," which was his way of describing Rod.

Naturally Ross and I also prayed with the fervor of those in distress. To our relief, we finally began to get letters from our son, describing his gradual recovery and hospital release.

Rod received the Combat Infantry Badge, Presidential Citation, CBI Campaign, with three combat stars. He was also given a Purple Heart with an Oak Leaf Cluster. But to us the greatest award was God's grace and protection. In thanks Ross and I decided to regularly help in the mission of our church.

*   *   *

No one can describe the joy we felt when Rod returned to us safe and sound from his incredible war adventures. The single year he had enlisted for had stretched into five, and it was a more serious and mature young man we now welcomed home. He enrolled at Arizona State University in Tempe to study business administration. Later he attended business college to enable himself to become an accountant.

One would hardly call Rod serious, however, during our little family reunion in the summer of 1945. Bill and Mary came out on their annual visit from Chicago, and it was wonderful to be together once more. The house was filled with music and laughter as we caught up on the events of each other's lives.

We knew how fortunate we were. Our hearts went out to our friends and relatives who had lost their dear ones in the conflict. To honor those alumni who had made the supreme sacrifice, the Phoenix Indian School employed Emry Kopta, a noted sculptor, to erect a memorial in front of the auditorium. A beautiful bronze plaque was engraved with the young soldiers' names as a lasting remembrance.

One Pima fighting boy, Ira Hamilton Hayes, participated in the planting of the American flag on Mount Suribachi, taking his place among those who have made history. The burden of fame proved heavy for Ira, who died near Bapchule in January 1955. Did we who bear the name of Christians miss our chance to help him in his distress?

My brother Bill had proved that the power of music could cut across racial barriers and help people to find themselves. It was up to us to prove the similar power of love. Love, along with a helping hand, should be extended to all our fellowmen, regardless of creed and national origin. We are, and must be, our brother's keepers.

A Helping Hand

MY DETERMINATION to conquer prejudice by proving that the American Indian is an asset to our nation gave me the courage to become active in a number of organizations with all-white memberships. During our years on Jackson Street many opportunities for such participation presented themselves.

Of course, Ross and I had always been involved in a certain amount of activities outside the home. Since the war he had been a member of the Veterans of World War I, and I had been a part of the World War I Apache Trails Auxiliary in Mesa. Most of our other outside interests had centered around the Central Presbyterian Indian Church across from the Phoenix Indian School, which we had attended regularly since before we were married. Although Jackson Street was four and one-half miles away from this church, we still drove the distance every Sunday morning to worship with our old friends.

But all of our activities had been in association with other Indians. Now we were faced with the challenge of being accepted in organizations composed mainly of whites. Would we fit in, or would the barrier of racial discrimination set us apart?

Our little son Billy was a good example for us to follow. He attended Jackson Elementary School and had never thought of himself as different from his white classmates. I brought to mind his childlike confidence when I attended my first PTA meeting.

It turned out that my doubts regarding prejudice had not been without grounds; at first some of the members did seem uncomfortable about having an Indian in the organization. However, the speaker for that day told a story with the moral that we were all part of one family, and from then on I felt that I was a wanted member of the group.

A neighbor asked me to be her assistant on the refreshment committee, and I began to call mothers each month to ask them to bring cookies and doughnuts to our meetings. At first I was a little afraid to act as a hostess and serve on the various committees, but my white friends had confidence in me, and I soon found my PTA work enjoyable and rewarding.

When Billy reached his ninth birthday, he became a Cub Scout. Many a time Ross, although tired from work, attended the evening meetings with us. We sat with other parents, watching our sons demonstrate their accomplishments. Sometimes the youngsters were given topics to discuss in groups. Our little boy was always chosen as spokesman to bring his team's report to us parents. It always made Ross and me feel so proud and thankful to hear our son's childish, extemporaneous speech.

*   *   *

In 1950 I began a two-year writer's course to enable myself to set down the ancient legends of our people in an interesting manner. This was all a part of my plan to help make both Indians and whites aware of the proud heritage of the original Americans.

My first major writing project was a play called *Darkness to Light,* which depicted the story of how Reverend Cook brought Christianity to the Pimas. It was performed very successfully at our church, and we used the proceeds to send needy children to Christian summer camp.

My greatest thrill was the fact that my brother Bill came from Chicago especially to see the drama. He corrected my spelling of Ross' great-grandmother's name, *S-oam Heosig* (Yellow Flowers), and his eyes sparkled with enthusiasm as he joined in the applause. After the play, he came up to me and took my hand. "It was a wonderful drama, sister," he said. It made me feel proud to think he had enjoyed my writing, even though I knew it was partly because he was my brother.

From then on, in the midst of my bustling life, whenever I had the time I wrote down the legends of my people. It was my hope to eventually put them together in a little book, but because of my busy schedule, I knew that it would take years to finish the project. Actually, I had started recording the Pima legends in 1930, when I first realized that they were fast being lost as our old people passed away. But now I had to rewrite them in a colorful style which readers of all races would enjoy.

Eighteen years were to pass before my dream of a published book of legends would come true, but during that time I received wonderful encouragement in my writing from the members of the United Church Women, an organization later to be known as the Church Women United. I had joined this group in the early 1940s, when a PTA board member invited me to accompany her to a meeting. My curious nature had prompted me to go to see a real ecumenical gathering at work.

Upon our arrival, my friend introduced me to the members. For the first time in my life, no one stared at my copper skin! What a relief it was not to be looked over like a piece of wood with no feelings!

I was not asked what church I attended. Instead I felt a genuine air of Christian fellowship. After several meetings, I decided to join this unusual organization.

The purpose of CWU was to "unite church women in their allegiance to their Lord and Savior Jesus Christ through a program, looking to their integration in the total life and work of the church and to the building of a world Christian community." The members followed this doctrine in a faithful and effectual way. Their sincerity made me realize that ecumenical awareness was what I had lacked in my own life. Social efforts were not enough. To truly help integrate the Indian, I must attend the CWU study sessions so I could offer a real helping hand in the building of a world united through God.

CWU was divided into three departments — Christian World Missions, Christian Social Relations, and Christian World Relations. After several years of service, I was elected to serve as second vice president and later vice president in the department of Christian World Missions. My special project was organizing our participation in the World Day of Prayer. There were packets to send for, committee meetings to plan, and workers to be chosen. These were heavy responsibilities for a novice, but the Christian women all helped me in my work.

World Day of Prayer is held on the first Friday in Lent. The observance started with one denomination but soon grew into an international effort, then became interdenominational. Prayers encircle the earth, from the rising of the sun on the Tonga Islands in the Pacific to its setting on Saint Lawrence Island near Alaska.

Readers, just think of the fervent prayers of men, women, and children kneeling in some 22,000 American communities in more than 145 areas of the world! How can anyone say that God is dead? He is alive today! His spirit lives in us! We will truly conquer prejudice through fellowship in the living God!

*   *   *

As the years went by I found more and more time for my ecumenical activities. Our little brood was leaving the nest. We watched them go with the mingled joy and sadness which is familiar to parents of every race and creed.

By the time of my brother Bill's visit in 1950 Adeline had already been married for four years to a fine Pima named Archie Russell. Soon we were the proud grandparents of six grandchildren: Ronald, Sandra, Vernon, Marvin, Loren, and Debra. Their Granduncle Bill once taught the little tykes where to find turtles in the Gila. By now our river was only a scantly flowing trickle compared to the wide stream of our childhood, but the turtles were still there, a nice reminder of the past.

Around this time our son Rod was working as an accountant for the BIA in Parker, Arizona. Later he would be transferred to the farming community of Saint Ignatius, Montana, and then to the city of Billings. Never in one place for long, our oldest son would then go on to the Crow Indian Agency in Montana, and finally become a traveling auditor out of Denver. Luckily his many travels did not keep him from frequently visiting Ross and me with his lovely Pima wife Selma and his two daughters, Shirley Ann and Monica Joyce.

Billy was an active and interested teenager during the early 1950s. He would not leave our little nest until 1956, when he married a Yavapai Apache girl named Geraldine and began a family of his own. He majored in history at Arizona State University with the eventual goal of teaching this subject in high school. At nights he would pore over his books while the three little ones romped about his apartment. We all admired his determination to get that degree.

Billy's namesake, my dear brother Bill Moore, brought tears to the eyes of all us Shaws when he died of leukemia in 1951. Little did I know that the night of my play's small triumph would be the last time I would see my brother well and happy!

Bill was buried near his loved ones in the cemetery at Gila Crossing, after a beautiful funeral service presided over by the Masonic Order. Rod and Adeline rendered the meditation from Massenet's opera *Thaïs* on the violin and piano their uncle had helped them learn to play. Tears flowed freely down my children's faces, and there wasn't a dry eye in the congregation when the sad strains of music faded away.

All deeply mourned the passing of this talented and generous musician who could have been great in his own right, but instead chose to give the gift of music to all who came to him. Bill was a great teacher and a great man; his memory will always be cherished by those who were privileged to know him. The memorial written by our nephew Everett, which appears in the Epilogue of this book, is a truly fitting tribute.

*   *   *

Reminiscences of my brother were the order of the day when Russell "Big Chief" Moore, his nephew and musical protégé, met me at the airport in New York in 1962. My work with the Church Women United had kept me going places. This was especially true after I was transferred to the department of Christian Social Relations. Assignment Race, a three-year project designed to ease prejudice toward minority groups in America, was right up my line. How thrilled I was to have the opportunity to contribute to this effort!

The need for such a project was illustrated when I attended a meeting regarding Assignment Race in San Francisco. My companions on this trip were a black and a white from Tucson. Once during our stay we were startled to see our black friend treated unjustly at a lunch counter. She conducted herself in an orderly fashion, but I felt pain for her sake. "My mother always told me never to return any mistreatment," she told us. But despite her politeness and good decorum, her eyes told us that she was hurt deeply.

My trip to New York occurred soon after this event. I felt so humble to be chosen by my dear friends for the honor. Never in my whole life had I dreamed of going to America's largest city! At first I was reluctant to embark

Russell "Big Chief" Moore, one of J. Newton's sons, became my brother Bill's ward and music student. From the beginning he had a burning interest in jazz, and his determination to play this kind of music, despite his various teachers' insistence on classical training, finally brought him to the big time. The story of his life, including his long career with Louis Armstrong's band, is told in the Epilogue of this book.

on the adventure, but the wonderful Christian women, especially our president Fran Luther inspired and encouraged me to go.

My companion for the voyage was the CWU press chairman from Tucson. Our slow plane seemed to stop in almost every city; soon our ears were hurting, and our stomachs were feeling queasy. How lucky we were to have a kind fellow like my nephew Russell to meet us at La Guardia Airport! He whisked us to his home on Long Island, where his Oneida Indian wife Ida prepared us a delicious lunch. Then he took us to the big city, where our seminar was to be held.

As we passed by the crowded skyscrapers which hid the dimly shining sun, I thought of the Pima name for a dense growth of mesquite on the Gila River Reservation — New York Thicket. Finally, sixty-four years after my birth near that grove of trees, I came to understand how truly appropriate that name was. The Pimas always loved to give names, and they were very good at it.

When our training for Assignment Race was over, I went to stay with Russ for another week. He insisted on this, for I had brought him a collection of Pima Indian foods, and he wanted me to cook them for him. After years of eating the white man's fare, the old tastes reminded him of his first home. Over and over he told me that he had never realized how much he missed the traditional delicacies, especially our little brown tepary beans, a native of the southwestern desert.

My nephew also insisted that I see the sights of his interesting part of the country. He took time from his busy schedule with Louis Armstrong's jazz band to take me on a boat cruise up the Hudson. It was a thrill to see the old gal, the Statue of Liberty, of whom I had read so often in my school books.

The gorgeous October leaves were something to behold. We passed near Washington Irving's home, the area around which was the setting for his famous stories, "Rip Van Winkle" and "The Legend of Sleepy Hollow." "Where are the Catskill Mountains where Rip slept for so many years?" I asked. When Russ pointed them out to me I was so surprised — they looked more like soft Huhugam mounds than the craggy Arizona mountains I was used to. Our guide then pointed out the area where Edgar Allan Poe had lived. In school I had liked reading Irving's lively stories better than the somber poetry of this author.

When my visit ended, Russell changed my plane ticket to allow me to fly by fast-traveling jet. My return journey by this mode of travel was much easier than the uncomfortable trip east had been.

Ross met me at the Phoenix airport, anxious to hear of my adventures and filled with news of his own. As I talked enthusiastically of Assignment Race, his quiet resignation dampened my spirits a bit. " Yes, we must fight it, Anna," he said, "but prejudice will always be here."

Would it be? During my trip to New York I had encountered only goodwill and enthusiasm for Christian fellowship. In my classes I had learned much that would enable me to help ease the misunderstandings which lead to discrimination. Despite my husband's words, I could see a day when people of all races and creeds would live together in brotherly love. I vowed to offer an even stronger helping hand toward the accomplishment of this goal.

A Return to Nature

MY TRIP TO NEW YORK turned out to be the culmination
of my urban life experiences. Even as my fast jet was wing-
ing its way back to Phoenix, Ross was overseeing the
closing transactions on the sale of our beautiful Jackson
Street home. Now that he had retired from ARE, my
husband's lifetime dream could finally be realized. With
happy excitement he made plans for our move back to
the Salt River Reservation Community where he had been
born and raised.

What a change — from New York City to New York
Thicket! My friends all wondered how I would adjust to
life in a rural atmosphere — I had been active in so many
organizations in Phoenix. I think they somehow pictured
Ross and me as going "back to the blanket."

What a foolish thought that was! Forty years of working
in the white man's world had taught us to appreciate
civilized comforts. Even before we left our Jackson Street
house, Ross was busy making plans for our reservation
residence.

My husband was sixty-eight years old by now, but his
well-built body was still active and strong. He purchased

Photo by Helga Teiwes-French, Arizona State Museum, Tucson

Pimas have always been farmers; I guess it is in their blood. Almost before our reservation house was completed, Ross was planting citrus trees and vegetables. Now we enjoy fresh things all summer; what we don't eat I can for our winter meals. In the spring, blossoming orange trees like this one fill our yard with fragrance.

a frame shell house and put it on a lovely desert lot in Victory Acres, a group of home sites set aside for Pima and Maricopa war veterans. His brothers and other relatives helped him finish the inside, and soon our new little home was quite comfortable. In time Ross built a living room addition, another bedroom, two storage sheds, and a wire fence to keep the neighbors' horses from trampling his vegetables.

Ross' concern for his garden was understandable — within no time after we were settled his juicy watermelons and home-grown vegetables had become a welcome part of our daily fare. Later he added grapes, citrus fruits, and apricots for me to can for winter meals. Ross has a green thumb; whatever he plants grows well, for he waters it regularly and cares for it with love.

During those first days after our return to Salt River, we would sometimes almost cry with happiness. After years in the city the sweet sounds of nature were such blessings! How beautifully the mockingbird sang for us each morning!

On summer nights, when the warm air was heavy with fragrances from Ross' garden, we would sit outside and see the heavens filled with the same stars our ancestors had gazed upon. So often on nights like that Ross would repeat to me, "Anna, it is true. God is taking care of us. All is coming the way I want it to."

I had to agree with him. At first I had had my doubts about returning to reservation life, but soon I knew that Ross had been right. We weren't going back to the blanket but back to nature. That was how we put it. This was our return to nature.

*   *   *

Of course, it wasn't long before I found myself involved in many organizations and activities. We immediately joined the Salt River Presbyterian Church, where Pima Indian pastor Edmund Nelson and his wonderful congregation welcomed us warmly. Even though we missed the Phoenix church we had attended for more than fifty years, we soon felt at home.

However, I was glad that I still occasionally saw some of my old Phoenix friends at meetings of the board of directors of the C. H. Cook Christian Training School. For a long time located near the Indian School, this institution was finally moved to a beautiful spot in Tempe. I was honored to be chosen to serve this fine school which had helped so many young Indians to become ambassadors for Christ.

Since 1958 I had been serving as an ordained elder of our Phoenix church. I had been the first woman to hold this honor; how touching it was to think that my fellow Christians placed so much trust in me! Shortly after my ordination they sent me to Purdue University to meet with church leaders from all over the world. It was an inspiring experience of Christian brotherhood.

Upon our return to the reservation, our new congregation also placed its confidence in us. Ross had more time now, so he joined me as an elder of the Salt River Presbyterian Church.

Our duties included the responsibility of visiting Presbyterians all over the reservation, offering comfort to the sick and bereaved and encouraging the people to attend Sunday services. What shock I felt at seeing the dirt and squalor of some of the homes I visited! Often the houses were in such poor condition that the roofs leaked, causing the plaster to fall from the ceilings. Frequently these badly maintained homes belonged to single elderly people, who could do nothing to effect the necessary repairs.

My heart went out to these poor old ones. In days gone by they would have been honored and cared for by their children. In return they would have watched over their grandchildren, who would bring them sunshine and laughter. There was no reason for Medicare or welfare programs in the old days; people looked after each other's needs.

What had we Pimas done to ourselves in adopting the white man's ways? Our old people now had to face life all alone, without help, love, or comfort. Their families were so often broken up and apart, with alcohol or drugs as the cause. Those couples who were still together frequently were busy making money in the cities, oblivious to the needs of their aged parents. Surely we owed these dear old people something!

My feelings of outrage were shared by my fellow volunteer workers on the Medicare Committee of the reservation's Community Action Program, then a component of the Office of Economic Opportunity. Many elderly Pimas and Maricopas were confused by Medicare, so we workers went out to their homes to explain the benefits of the program and enroll all who qualified. Some of the oldsters we visited poured their hearts out to us, but others would not even invite us in, so ashamed were they of their wretched shacks.

We reported our findings to our supervisor Merlin Schurz. He was filled with sympathy when he heard how our neglected old ones needed their wood chopped, yards cleaned, roofs repaired, and mud walls plastered. Some wanted a garden spaded, while others needed transportation to the clinic or supermarket. All of them yearned for a little human contact to brighten their long, lonely days.

A fellow Medicare volunteer named Myra Rice suggested that we have a luncheon for the "cute, sweet ladies," as she called them. During the course of eating we could evaluate the true situation and think about assembling a report. The potluck meal took place in one aged woman's small adobe, and everyone enjoyed the delicious food and good talk. The old people aired their problems and felt much the better for it.

After preparing our report, we marched to the Community Action Program Office to request that an "Aid to the Elderly" program be created. Using CAP funds we could pay our young people to transport the old ones to the doctor or the store and do their chores for them. Volunteers could be organized to make regular visits to the lonely.

This was how the Aid to the Elderly Program began. Since its inception in 1966 it has been a boon to our poor old people, so many of whom had been forgotten in a changing world. More must be done, to be sure, but this program is a step in the right direction.

*   *   *

Counting my years in school, I had lived almost fifty years in Phoenix. Yet I had never forgotten my Pima blood and my proud Indian heritage. Now that I was back on the reservation, I was finding many opportunities to revive our precious Pima past and bring it to life once more.

Soon after our return Ross saw a funny example of my revival of traditions. For months I had been thinking of those years of my childhood, when I spent hours and hours grinding wheat and parched corn on the worn metate. The thought of the oldtime delicacies made my mouth water, but was it worth the sore knees and blistered hands? Then my ingenuity came to the fore — why not wear gloves and put the metate on a table? How Ross laughed when he saw me grinding in this manner! Well, he could laugh all he wanted — it certainly was more comfortable, and I didn't notice him refusing the old-fashioned pinole and tortillas I made from the wheat.

Another revival of traditions, more true to the old ways than the grinding, has been done in conjunction with a group we call *Whahathum* (Pima Basket-Weavers). The group was formed when a number of concerned women began to notice that the intricate basket-weaving art of our ancestors was slowly dying out.

From times immemorial this treasured talent has been passed lovingly from one generation to the next. But most modern youngsters just don't have the time or interest to learn such a painstaking skill. We decided to organize women's weaving classes under the tutelage of those great artists who are still left, so that this proud heritage will be preserved for the generations to come.

My mother had been a master weaver. Her gnarled fingers were never idle, for every moment of her leisure time was dedicated to the creation of magnificent baskets like the one pictured in this book. Now I wish I had spent more time learning her wonderful skill. She had been willing to teach, but I was always too busy with my family duties and outside activities.

In her place I now have such renown basket-weavers as Hilda Manuel and Mary Sampson. They are patient

Photo by Helga Teiwes-French, Arizona State Museum, Tucson

Ross' mother made this basket, which I treasure in my collection. Before the white man came, Pima basket designs were all abstract geometric patterns. Then the traders encouraged us to add animals and people, as in Ross' mother's design. They said their white customers liked them better this way.

and kindly teachers, always anxious to help our group in our efforts to preserve the proud art of our ancestors.

First they showed us how to gather and prepare the willow, devil's claw, and cattail. Gathering procedures are quite different than they were in my Aunt Dawn's day, when desert weeds grew abundantly around the Pima villages. As the years have passed the white man has all but obliterated the natural vegetation with his agriculture and subdivisions. So we modern-day weavers must actually cultivate willow trees and devil's claws in our gardens!

As we work the hard-won materials into treasured baskets under the exacting eyes of our expert teachers, we talk of many things. Our group is interesting in that it includes several white women, all of whom think and act more like Pimas in their serious concern for preserving a dying Indian heritage.

In the early days of our group, one prime interest was researching the origin of the ancient designs. Our work took us into museums and libraries, and the subject of museums arose. We all agreed that if our Pima-Maricopa heritage was to be truly preserved we would have to create a museum on the Salt River Reservation. From meeting to meeting we talked and planned while our fingers slowly formed the weeds into the beautiful old designs.

Oddly enough, a major problem was finding artifacts with which to stock a museum. For years the poverty-stricken Pimas had been forced to market their wonderful handicrafts to the white man in order to buy groceries for their families. I thought of the many beautiful baskets my mother had sold for as little as fifty cents each and remembered the huge clay ollas she had made for the church to sell for one dollar apiece. Because of such dealings, most examples of fine old Pima artistry were now in the hands of the white man. How ironic that seemed to me!

But at last we basket-weavers had a stroke of luck. Byron Harvey of the Fred Harvey Foundation offered to sell his collection of fine Pima baskets to us for our museum. But how would we find the funds to buy it? The busy and determined women of our group set to work and at last obtained a grant from William S. King, who realized the importance of the museum project. The beautiful baskets which had been woven so skillfully by our ancestors were finally restored to us! Our dream of a Pima-Maricopa museum was about to become a reality!

The articles of incorporation of the Salt River Pima-Maricopa Indian Arts & Crafts, Inc., were signed on April 12, 1972. A building was assigned to our use until the tribal civic center, complete with a new museum, was completed.

Besides the Harvey Collection, our museum displays many additional baskets and a wide variety of pots, grinding stones, pictures, and ancient artifacts. All of these items have been donated from the personal collections of many friends across the reservation. A new pride in our heritage is evident as Pimas and Maricopas see the relics of their great past and hear the admiring comments from visitors of all races.

When the new museum has been completed, it will have a gift shop, where the Indian people can place their handiwork on sale. The quality of these items will rival that of old, for the museum will offer free lessons in the ancient arts, crafts, and culture to all who want to learn.

As we basket-weavers walk the aisles of the museum, admiring the fine displays, we find it difficult to believe that all this began with the hopes and plans of a few concerned ladies not so very long ago. At times when we feel discouraged about the many other problems and needs of our Indian community, we can look to this project for inspiration. It shows us what can be done with a little pride and determination. Surely the time is not far away when our Indian race will walk the trail of success!

*   *   *

Finding the trail of success by facing our problems with wisdom and courage is a major theme of our Pima newsletter *Awathm Awahan (Pima Letters)*, which I edited for three years. In order to solve our difficulties we must be aware of them, and we do not skip lightly over serious issues in the pages of this monthly news organ. Stories discussing the activities of the BIA, the Tribal Council, the Community Action Program, the Land Board, and various community committees are frequent.

But the pages of *Awathm Awahan* are not confined to the serious. Pimas love sports, and news of the various events is always looked forward to. Basketball games with both male and female teams attract big crowds to the Pi-Copa Gym. In the summer swimming competition in the pool is big news, and the annual baseball tournament, with interstate teams representing all tribes, always gets a headline.

Personal news of our friends and neighbors also has big billing. This, along with reports of club activities, keeps the columns of our newsletter lively and interesting. My

The modernistic Pi-Copa recreational complex is a good symbol of the progress we see coming to the Salt River Reservation. The air-conditioned building features full sports and playground facilities, an olympic-sized swimming pool, offices, and rooms for adult education, kindergarten, and day-care classes.

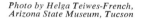

Photo by Helga Teiwes-French,
Arizona State Museum, Tucson

thanks are due to the many energetic young associate editors who helped me make *Awathm Awahan* what it is today.

The appearance in our newsletter of more and more items regarding educational opportunities in Salt River is indicative of an increasing interest in self-improvement on the part of many Pimas and Maricopas. Education, of course, is the answer to many of the problems which exist in the Indian communities.

Since Ross' and my return to the reservation we have seen the establishment of so many wonderful educational programs. For adults, these include vocational training classes, Indian culture appreciation classes, and instruction in the various household arts. For our children there

are kindergarten and day-care classes. I have become active in teaching the little ones who attend them.

It was a thrill when the Community Action Program invited me to teach the youngsters the old legends and songs in the Pima tongue. I was excited to have the opportunity to contribute to a program designed to preserve our Indian identity. These days most of our children speak but one language — English. When we talk to them in Pima, their little faces look blank. We do not blame their parents one bit; so often they have married into other tribes and found it necessary to use a common language. English serves this purpose well, and, of course, it is the dominant tongue of the United States. How Ross and I struggled to learn it!

Now, however, we must retrieve our Pima heritage before it is lost completely. Teaching little children the old language is one important first step toward this goal. Most of my classes are at the kindergarten level, but the little tots at the day-care center enjoy the lessons too. All of the youngsters love to learn to count in Pima and to say the names of the various animals. One morning a little boy followed me to the door and said proudly, "Goodbye, *judum* (bear)!" I was so amused; in his young eyes did I look like a bear? I smiled and quipped back, "Goodbye, *ban* (coyote)!"

In general tiny children are not bashful about speaking the language and learn easily. I have become more and more convinced that the place to begin to teach Indian culture is the kindergarten classroom. If we do not begin this early, the tots lose their childish enthusiasm and later on find the Pima tongue strange and odd-sounding. A good example of this is our own grandson Bradford, who has had no opportunity to learn the Pima language in his home. When he comes to visit us and Ross sings the old Pima songs, he runs into the bedroom and laughs. No wonder — the words sound so very different from his familiar English!

*   *   *

In recent days we have seen more and more of little Bradford and his brother and sister. In the midst of our happy return to nature, the shadow of death has crossed our lives. Our dear son Bill, the youngest of our brood, was suddenly taken from us in April 1968.

One moment he was working at his desk — then came that fateful study break which ended in a fatal beating.

Only now can I understand the pain Red Arrow must have felt upon the passing of his beautiful Juana. Like my father, I have found comfort and strength in Jesus Christ, our Lord and King.

Bill was taken during his final semester at Arizona State University. He had already been accepted as a history teacher at a Phoenix high school. His whole life was before him; his death seemed so cruel and senseless.

Ross and I have tried to help by caring for the children whenever we can. The oldest, Billy Junior, lives with us and commutes to Westwood High School in Mesa. Good-natured and reliable, he gets up at 5:30 A.M. to prepare his own breakfast and catch the bus to school. He does all his own washing and ironing and still finds time to play on our Salt River basketball team and pursue school sports activities.

The two youngest, Karen Rose and Bradford Layne, live in a house near us. Their mother has remarried and, like so many modern young parents, works outside the home. Ross and I look forward to the frequent visits of the youngsters, during which we talk often of their father to keep his image alive for them.

Ross plays with little Bradford while I teach Karen to crochet, and the sounds of youthful laughter fill our home. However, there are still moments of sadness when we see our Bill's features reflected in his children's eager young faces.

*   *   *

A happier event of our retirement was our fiftieth anniversary celebration on June 5, 1970. Rod and Adeline cooked it up, inviting all of our old friends to a great hemapig, or gathering, at the Salt River Presbyterian Church. Our little wedding had been so simple — finally after fifty years we were going to celebrate in style!

Ross and I felt overwhelmed when we saw so many of our dear friends brought together. It was strange to see more white faces than Indian, but then more than forty years of our marriage had been spent in Phoenix, and we had made many cherished friends there.

This is not to imply that the Indians were not well represented. We were especially touched to see our dear school chum, the famous Maricopa potter Ida Redbird. In the course of the program my children had organized, the choir sang Ida's favorite hymn as a special tribute to her. What a happy lady she was! To us it seemed like such a little thing compared to the years of inspiration her beautiful soprano voice and wonderful skill in ceramics had given us.

After the program there was a great feast in true Pima hemapig style. Our guests enjoyed a rich array of delicious traditional foods: Indian stew, tortillas, tamales, roast of beef. Jean Ann, daughter of my dear sister-in-law Jennie, helped Adeline hostess the affair, and another relative, Elizabeth King, made us a huge decorated cake. Ross and I were on top of the world as we reminisced with our wonderful old friends, teachers, and relatives.

We were especially touched to see a great table laden with gifts. Ross reminded me of the two sets of dishes which had been our sole wedding presents. "It's fifty years late, but here is your wedding shower!" he quipped.

*   *   *

When our guests had all departed, Ross and I sat alone, sharing the happiness of the day. What a variety of friends we had been blessed with! They represented all races and creeds, all classes and educational levels. Upon seeing them enjoy each other together at our party, one would feel that prejudice had surely been conquered. I knew that this was not yet so, but my husband and I had seen great progress in the course of our lifetimes.

Science has confirmed that there is no one superior race. Skin colors may be different, but the same red blood flows in the veins of all racial groups. Let us once and for all tear down the barriers that keep people from truly knowing their neighbors! Let everyone be as free of prejudice as that group of fine guests at our fiftieth anniversary party!

Pima Progress

BACK IN 1920 when Ross and I were hopeful young newly-weds, we had but two alternatives — farming in wretched poverty on the reservation or working hard to get ahead at a city job in the white man's world. We, of course, chose the latter, but in doing so we had to give up the opportunity to be with other Indians on our own land and share in our proud Pima-Maricopa heritage. We had to live like white men.

Only when we were pensioners, receiving monthly checks from off-reservation sources, could we afford to return to the land of our birth. Now we are working to develop the reservation in such a way that Indians of the future generations will have more than the two stark choices that were open to Ross and me.

When the white man set up the reservation system, it was based on the premise that discovery of Indian lands by Europeans gave them the right to absolute title to them. The Indian was considered merely an occupant of those areas which the white man chose to set aside for him. He could not sell or lease reservation lands without the permission of the true owner, the United States government.

How unfair all this seems today! When the first boatload of non-Indians landed on the Atlantic shores, the original inhabitants extended a helping hand to the strangers. Later, when the white man's canvas-covered wagons began to roll over the narrow, rough trails of the Arizona desert, the noble Pima was there to welcome him, feed him, and quench his thirst with huge clay ollas of cool water. How different it would have been if the Massachusetts Indians had chosen to sink the Mayflower or if the Pimas had attacked the wagons with war clubs and arrows! But our forefathers were meek and generous, ready to help all those in distress.

What thanks did they get for their kindness? Their ancient lands were taken from them, and they were placed in a state of dependency, like children. This injustice continued until 1887, when an act was finally passed allowing individual ownership of small land allotments on the reservations. At last the Indian was to be treated as a responsible adult. Each allottee would have full title to his land — he could keep it, sell it, lease it, or dispose of it as he saw fit.

In 1910 Ross received a small parcel of allotment land on the sandy riverbed near the place of his birth. At one time worth almost nothing, this land has shot up in value as the white man's subdivisions have developed around it. Now, as chairman for all allottees in his area, Ross is negotiating with a developer who is erecting a mobile home park there. The Indian owners are setting the terms themselves and reaping large profits from their little plots. In earlier days they would have had no such right.

Of course, non-allotment reservation lands are still held in trust by the United States government. For years we were limited to short-term leasing of these areas to outsiders. With this restriction, how could we encourage industrial and commercial development with any success? A renter on a twenty-five year lease is bound to be wary of his greenbacks, so impermanent is the security of his investment.

The 1966 bill which gave Indians the right to offer ninety-nine year leases for reservation lands heralded the rosy dawn of a new era. Now we could begin to make long-term plans for molding our desert lands into carefully planned communities through ninety-nine year leasing for diverse development.

The Salt River General Development Plan was the Pima-Maricopa response to this new opportunity. Our tiny farms which had for years been let to white farmers for small amounts of cash could finally be utilized in an efficient manner.

To help us develop our new concept, we called in Simon Eisener and Associates, planning consultants. In a polite and soft-spoken manner, Mr. Eisener presented us with a large map, showing broad, sweeping streets with green trees, flowers, and shrubbery in the middle. On the map, the idle desert land between the Arizona Canal and the McDowell Mountains had been transformed into several areas of development. In the center was a thickly populated urban area with schools, churches, commercial plants, and homes. Nearby were low-density residential sections for wealthy people and perhaps a movie colony. There was a manmade lake with recreational cabins and a golf course west of Sawik, the Red Mountain, for all to enjoy.

Sawik itself was to be preserved as a natural, unde-veloped area for future generations. For years this moun-tain has had special meaning to the Indians, who sur-rounded it with legend and song. Red in color like the red men, it resembles a chief taking care of his people.

At first the Eisener plan was a puzzle to many of our older residents. They were left blinking their eyes at the fast pace of time − the white man's time, whose pressure soon causes nervous breakdowns and ulcers.

"We don't know about all these modern ideas," the old ones repeated and repeated. "Our ancestors learned that it is good to take time to meditate, to know what you want and where you are going. Only then should you do it very slowly, thus making fewer errors. Our forebears lived to the ripe old ages of ninety-five or one hundred by going at this quiet pace. Now you want us to quickly adopt a strange new plan like Mr. Eisener's. What would our ancestors say?"

It was hard to convince the oldtimers of the truth of *"Vh-Thaw-Hup-Ea-Ju"* ("It Must Happen"), as our rela-tives on the Gila River Reservation had been saying for a number of years. Now that we had the ninety-nine year lease it was necessary to take advantage of the benefits it could bring pronto.

To further persuade the reluctant members of our com-munity, members of the Tribal Council, the BIA, and several guests, including myself, boarded a light plane to visit the Agua Caliente band of Mission Indians in Palm Springs, California. At one time these people had been among the poorest of American Indians. Then came the ninety-nine year lease and the development of a community plan similar to the one now proposed to us.

We were amazed to see the checkerboard home area, where an Indian's lot stood next to a non-Indian's. The fabulous Hotel Spa, constructed on a long-term lease, was an asset which had helped this poverty-stricken band become one of the wealthiest Indian groups in California. As a contrast, we saw the buildings in the industrial park, which had been constructed on twenty-five year leases. Many were badly in need of repairs; the owners weren't willing to put money into a short-term investment.

Our report of what we saw in Palm Springs helped convince the opponents of the Eisener plan. It was enthusiastically adopted, and it promises to bring a new prosperity to the Pima and Maricopa people.

*   *   *

The Salt River General Development Plan is only one part of the modern effort to make our reservation a better place to live. Our young people should not be forced to move to the cities in order to maintain a decent standard of living. Proper planning and development can bring good jobs and civilized comforts to the reservation itself, where young Indians can enjoy the advantages of both worlds.

It would be impossible to give a full survey of the many projects being undertaken to achieve this new kind of reservation life. Modern Indian communities are alive with plans and activities. One of the most encouraging things about almost all the new efforts is the presence of active, interested Indian leadership. This is a real switch from the old days, when Indians were universally treated like savages or babies.

Since the passing of the Wheeler - Howard Act in 1934, most tribes have instituted tribal constitutions and tribal governments. That the Indians have been able to once again rule themselves after so many years of forced dependency on the white man is a tribute to their ancient heritage. Long ago Indians may not have had the white man's learning, but they were able to use their thinking and reasoning powers to form a nearly perfect democratic government. Now they are being given the chance to make their own decisions once again.

Our own Pima-Maricopa Tribal Council is a successful governing body. Over the years it has given rise to an organized tribal bureaucracy, including a number of important councils and committees. Most major posts are filled by Indians, and the Indian is being given more and more voice in the U.S. government agencies in charge of Indian affairs, including the BIA.

One good example of dedicated Indian leadership was the full-scale involvement of Salt River residents in the construction of a new youth center for neglected children of broken homes. At that time BIA and tribal funds were running low, but this was no obstacle to the determined Indians.

Reservation churches sponsored dinners and sold Indian food in booths. Individual families gave money. Some of us informed the civic and religious organizations in surrounding communities of our great need, collecting donations whenever possible.

When all had been gathered, it was evident that the

Our Salt River Youth Home proves that Pimas of today can work together to achieve a goal just as their ancestors did. Almost everyone in our community pitched in to build this modern version of the traditional saguaro-rib-and-mud house. Huge mesquite posts support the roof; the fireplace is lined with soft, shiny rocks from the Salt River. There is a modern kitchen, and the children enjoy bright, airy rooms. What a wonderful blending of the best of the old and the new!

funds were simply not adequate to finance the construction of a professionally contracted building in the white man's style. But still the Indians persisted in their dream.

What would be wrong with a home built of saguaro ribs caulked with mud in the old Pima manner? With diligence the Pimas and Maricopas scoured the desert for large mesquite posts. The once-plentiful supply had dwindled to almost nothing, due to the sale of big bundles of fragrant-burning mesquite wood to the white man during hard times. Other supplies had to be bought from the sparse funds, which constantly needed replenishing.

Work proceeded slowly but surely in the brutal summer heat. Afternoon temperatures went as high as 115 degrees, but the hardy Indians were undaunted.

Finally all was finished but the plastering of the walls.

The men prepared the traditional mixture of mud and straw, but the plastering itself had always been women's work. Where would we find women of today with the skill and patience to work with the sticky plaster? Then someone thought of the old people we on the Medicare Committee had been contacting daily. Surely some of these women would come through!

The jokes and laughter of that plastering day will long remain in my memory. The aged ladies turned out in force, anxious to show off their old art. "You women look too fancy in your modern clothes!" teased one old man. "You should be wearing squaw wraparounds like the plasterers of long ago!" All the women giggled at the idea.

When at last the youth center was finished, we surveyed our building with pride. It was so straight and perfect! We

Photos by Helga Teiwes-French, Arizona State Museum, Tucson

Like our olas kih of long ago, the beautiful Mutual Self-Help homes on the Gila and Salt River reservations are being built by the Indians themselves. This project is different from the typical government "handout" program in that it encourages learning and initiative. The pictures show Indian construction workers and their finished products — modern homes with well-kept yards reflecting the pride of their owners.

had started with nothing but willing hearts and hands. Yet these things had been enough: despite the blistering sun, we had made our dream a reality.

The dedication of the youth center took place at our traditional Indian Thanksgiving celebration, the Saturday before the national holiday. Invitations were sent to all the white leaders who had helped us collect funds for our project. Prominent cartoonist Reg Manning took advantage of the occasion by depicting a Pima man in Pilgrim's clothes offering a platter of turkey to the local paleface chiefs dressed in gaudy war bonnets. The drawing was captioned, "It's a switch."

As editor of our Pima newsletter, I found the cartoon food for thought. The unity, involvement, and cooperation which the youth center project had stimulated were deeply inspiring. When all mankind has learned to share and work together in this way, perhaps we can truly begin to think about an end to prejudice. After the races have come to live in brotherhood — then and only then can we have a real Reg Manning turnabout!

*   *   *

The same sort of Indian leadership and unified response to challenge were characteristic of the Mutual Self-Help Housing Program on the Salt and Gila River reservations. For five years I served on the all-Indian Salt River Housing Authority Commission in this regard, and it was a thrill to share in the excitement and pride of my relatives and tribesmen.

The purpose of the Mutual Self-Help Housing Program is to provide good homes for our low-income residents. With the aid of funds from the U.S. government, any

Indian who qualifies can obtain the building materials necessary to construct a solid, concrete-block, three-bedroom house. However, unlike the many Indian "handout" programs, Self-Help Housing requires that the future owner actually participate in the building of his new dwelling!

Of course the novice builder is offered help from trained construction workers and contractors. So in the end he not only has his beautiful new home but also has obtained the gifts of know-how, initiative, and pride in accomplishment. These characteristics help him to keep his home clean and neat and to meet his bills on time, the first important requirements of every home-owner.

We on the Mutual Self-Help Housing Authority Commission have been greatly aided by the all-Indian Water Committee, which works hard to see that precious water is piped to each new reservation home. No longer do we see horse-drawn wagons bringing water in rusty milkcans and barrels for our domestic use. The new houses have all the modern conveniences, including evaporative coolers and inside plumbing. What a contrast to the rough brush olas kih dwellings of my childhood!

Many of our more prosperous Indians have received FHA loans, and their houses equal those of wealthy non-Indians. Some have telephones, color television sets, stereos, and automatic washers. Many have more than one car parked in their yards. No longer must reservation-dwellers resign themselves to poverty-level living. Progress and prosperity at last are coming to Pima land!

Of course, to maintain the fine homes there must be good jobs and good paychecks. Many modern householders commute to nearby communities, where they are employed as superintendents, teachers, and clerical and industrial workers. But long daily drives can be expensive and tiring. So modern imagination and effort are going into creating good jobs for Indians right here on the reservation.

Some such projects, like the Tri-Community Landfill, benefit the tribe in many ways. Under this program, we rent land to the cities of Mesa and Scottsdale, which help pay Indians to excavate holes and compact refuse. In addition, we sell surplus sand and gravel for "gravy" income. Profits from this project have enabled us to buy expensive heavy equipment and add new Indian employees to the roster.

Of course, when the commercial and industrial complexes of the Salt River General Development Plan have been completed, many similar projects will be hatched. A number of them will employ women as well as men, for the dawn of women's liberation can be seen in our Salt River community.

Mothers who were not so long ago forced onto the rolls of welfare now have good-paying jobs due to our reservation's day-care center, financed by the Community Action Program. Pima and Maricopa women are registered nurses, nurses' aides, secretaries, and industrial workers. Interestingly, they earn especially high praises for their abilities to perform intricate, highly skilled jobs, such as diamond-cutting. Perhaps their nimble fingers and tireless patience are inherited from their basket-weaving ancestors.

*   *   *

Sometimes as I go through the rounds of my daily activities I wonder what our ancestors would think if they could observe the life of a modern-day Pima. What changes they would see! Imagine what my patient Great-grandmother Red Flowers would think of the hot, sudsy water swirling about in my automatic washer! Think of how strange our long friendly peace with other tribes would seem to my fierce Great-granduncle Turtle!

Our ancestors' lots were tough. The men raised their crops with one hand and stopped enemy raids with the other, while the women worked day and night gathering wild foods, carrying wood and water, and weaving. Although I have long strived to preserve our old Pima ways, the poverty, grueling work, and bloody battles are things I do not miss!

Our reservation life today is varied, rich, and rewarding. Each morning Ross can be found cleaning the yard, trimming the trees, mowing the lawn, or working in his garden. What a joy it is for him to pick the yellow grapefruit and juicy navel oranges for our table and for our friends! Our grape vines are extra-heavy bearers, and there are always apricots to give away.

While my husband works outside, I cook, wash the dishes, vacuum, dust, or do the laundry. Ross generally helps me hang the clothes. Then at one o'clock he drives to Scottsdale to pick up our mail.

Neighbors, friends, and relatives drop in frequently. Our home is always opened to people of every race, creed, and origin. From our living room come the sounds of three languages — Pima, Spanish, and English — and my kitchen steams with the good smells of both Indian and non-Indian foods.

As the last part of my story has shown, both Ross and I are busy with a wide range of activities outside our home.

First, of course, there is our church work. Besides the Sunday services, we go to prayer meeting every Wednesday. On days we cannot attend, we have our own prayers at bedtime.

On Thursdays I help the church women make quilts for money-raising sales; on Friday evenings my fingers are busy weaving Pima baskets. Once a month we attend the veterans' and women's auxiliary meetings in Mesa. In addition, of course, there are my daily kindergarten classes in Pima language and culture, as well as our many special projects for the betterment of the tribe. Ross is often at my side in the latter endeavors.

Our two surviving children, eleven grandchildren, and eight great-grandchildren also serve to keep us busy. All of the adults hold responsible jobs or go to college, but they still find time for Ross and me.

Adeline's six children are employed in a variety of interesting capacities in Phoenix. Three have taken up medically related careers: Ron is a psycho-technician, Sandra a registered nurse, and Marvin works for a surgical supply house. The other three are in school. Vernon is studying civil engineering, Loren is majoring in law enforcement, and Debra is learning interior decoration. The older ones have married upstanding members of various tribes, and all are well adjusted to life in the white man's world.

Rod's two girls have both attended college. Shirley has received her B.A., married a fine non-Indian, and gone to work for the BIA business administration. Monica is a secretary at the C. H. Cook Christian Training School.

The chatter of these active grandchildren keeps us up with the changing attitudes and ideas of modern youth.

We are proud of their intelligence and their readiness to reason for themselves. Yet like all young people, they sometimes make unwise decisions. Certainly Ross and I did the same. We oldsters try to keep our mouths closed unless counseling is asked for; sometimes one must make mistakes in order to learn.

*   *   *

I never dreamed that a feeling of sadness would overcome me as I finished writing this book. How, in fact, can I finish? With each passing day my Pima present melts into and becomes a part of my Pima past. Yet I cannot write on forever! Already I'm afraid I have sounded too much like my old coyote friend Ban.

So how shall I end my narrative? Insofar as it is possible, I would like to put into a nutshell the things I have learned in my lifetime of treading the bridge between two cultures. I am sure that in the course of this writing I have already voiced many of these thoughts, but I humbly believe that it is important to set these ideas down just once more, with everything brought together in one place.

The theme of my message is brotherhood. We all belong to one human family created by God. No race is superior or inferior; we are all brothers beneath the skin. It has been the main purpose of my life to conquer the barriers of prejudice which divide one race from another.

Naturally my efforts have centered on the cause of the American Indian. For too long the native American has been exploited and treated like a child. For too long he has seen his land dwindle away, his beautiful mountains and streams marred.

The white man's treatment of us has too often been selfish, unfair, inhumane, and cruel. Such treatment has had its predictable results — poverty, dependency, and, worst of all, a loss of pride in ourselves as Indians.

As long as native Americans continue to see themselves through the eyes of a prejudiced white — as childish, incapable, bestial, and stupid — they cannot take the first step in the battle against discrimination. Before we do anything else we must realize the great truth that we are not inferior, as some whites would have us believe, but people of great dignity and wisdom — friendly, generous, and always ready to help when any need arises.

The time has come to take pride in our Indian blood and our precious heritage. Our ancestors were not wild savages but a very religious people with a rich and varied culture. The white man was quick to make use of our vast knowledge of nature — many of the foods we eat today were derived from original Indian foods. But beyond our material culture we have our precious values, philosophies, artifacts, legends, songs, and dances to contribute to the world. Again I have the temerity to repeat: the first step for every Indian is the attainment of pride — a pride in himself and his wonderful heritage from the past.

But what of the present? The olas kih was ingenious, and we are proud of its history, but who among us desires to live that way today? To achieve the material comforts and cultural enrichments of the modern world, we must rise up and make good within its system, not fight it with violent tactics no better than those the white man once used on us. Bitterness only buttresses racial barriers. We too can be politicians, administrators, teachers, and leaders in all walks of life. We need only pride, confidence, experience, and, most important, education.

Education is the golden key to success for all people. In a nutshell, it teaches us service to others, patience, determination, understanding, and compassion. It enables the American Indian to value his heritage and use it for the benefit of others, to stick to his job and not be a quitter, to budget his time and money for the future, to have the poise and ability to express himself to others.

The list of education's benefits is, in truth, unending. But I would like to finish my little list with what I consider to be the greatest benefit of all — interracial understanding. Ignorance is prejudice's greatest ally. Once we understand another race's culture — once we have read its great books, listened to its music, and learned its philosophy and ideas — prejudice melts away like desert snow. Our minds are broadened, and our eyes are opened. Education, the key to success, is also the key to brotherly love.

I, of course, also believe in the message of brotherly love preached to us by our Lord Jesus Christ. Religious training was a gift Ross and I gave our youngsters along with the benefits of education in our modern culture. But perhaps in their involvement with the white man's schooling, they missed the opportunity to absorb the ways of the Indian.

Oh, I tried to teach them the Pima language and legends, but in the midst of the bustle of Phoenix, this all must have seemed so irrelevant. Rod only learned Pima when he returned to the reservation on vacations to help his grandparents. Adeline has never learned it.

Sacaton girls Collette Antone and Marie Jackson relax outside Collette's new Mutual Self-Help home. The better standard of living we see coming to our Pima-Maricopa reservations allows young people like these to enjoy the comforts of the white man's world without giving up the opportunity to live with other Indians and share in our proud heritage.

I am proud of Archie and Adeline. He works for the Phoenix Water Department, and now that the youngsters are grown, Adeline is working as a teacher's aide, hoping to go back to college for her teaching certificate. Her children are fine citizens; we love them all. But few members of my daughter's family have much interest in the old Pima-Maricopa heritage; they only return to the reservation to visit Ross and me. We are hoping this will change; lately Adeline herself has been showing a desire to learn the Pima tongue.

Our son Rod needs no convincing. He loves the old Pima foods and has never forgotten the language. When he retires from his auditing job he will return to the Salt River Community to make his home near us in Victory Acres.

This sort of feeling for the past is what I would hope for all American Indians. Education in the white man's world is enriching and essential to economic success, but it need not mean the giving up of our proud Pima heritage. All around us we are seeing a greater realization of this truth. Perhaps as more and more of our young people find good jobs on the reservations they will discover new ways to blend the two cultures into a way of life that is uniquely Indian.

Tremendous progress has already been made. The time is not too far off when racial brothers will understand each other with respect and reverence for the unusual qualities and differences which set them apart. When that day comes, we too with joy can say, "And the desert shall rejoice, and blossom as the rose."

Epilogue

Photo by Helga Teiwes-French

Anna Moore Shaw, 1973

My Indian Hall of Fame

How I WISH I COULD round out my narrative with the fascinating life stories of all the numerous individuals who have aided and inspired me in the course of my Pima past. But I have been blessed with the friendship of so many great people! I am forced to make choices; whom should I single out?

Perhaps the best criterion is cultural adjustment — I will include here those whose lives have shed special light on the process of bridging the gap between two cultures and living together in brotherly love. Because of the limits of space, I must still neglect many dear friends and relatives who have indeed contributed much in these areas. They are all so kind and encouraging; surely they will understand and forgive me.

I have entitled this section "My Indian Hall of Fame," but this does not mean that all the individuals described here are Indians or even famous in the sense of worldly recognition. Some are well known, while others are celebrated only by me; some are Indians, while one is a non-Indian who has thought more like an Indian and contributed significantly to our Indian culture.

Here then, is a short collection of biographies and vignettes. May they complement and add to the story of my life, promoting yet deeper understanding of our great Pima past.

A.M.S.

Wasaja: Dr. Carlos Montezuma

IN CENTRAL ARIZONA there is a mountain range on the south end of which Mother Nature has roughly formed four sharp peaks. The Pimas of old called the range the *Mazatzal* (Snaggle Teeth); the white man named the south end Four Peaks.

When I gaze at the majestic Four Peaks from my Salt River home, the events of a long-ago saga parade before me. I think of the little Apache lad named *Wasaja* (Beckoning), who was taken prisoner by the Pimas in 1872 at a place called Black Mesa under the shadow of Four Peaks.

Mixed emotions of heartache and joy overwhelm me when I picture the boy's mother. What if he had been my small son? The Apache woman never saw her little Wasaja after he was taken from her at the tender age of five, and she did not live to learn the incredible destiny her boy was to follow.

Wasaja's unfortunate mother must have put her son to bed with the usual tender words that fateful night in 1872. Probably she and her friends had to quiet snickering and call a halt to pranks before their children finally went to sleep; it was summer, and they had walked for miles to this mountainous place to gather the sweet mescal shoots, which were just right for roasting. The excitement of the temporary camp and the anticipation of the delicious roasted *a'ut* always put everyone in a holiday mood.

The Pima braves who saw the Apache wickiups, which had grown up like mushrooms beside the flowing creek, were not so merry. Their hearts were filled with the bitterness of revenge for the painful personal losses and crop failures they had suffered due to Apache raids. As soon as they had found a moment free from their fields they had headed for these mountains, for they knew that the Apaches, just like the Pimas themselves, could not resist the temptation of mescal ripe for roasting. Surely this area would be the place to find a poorly protected party of Apache squaws and children out gathering the delicacy. Pima revenge would be quick and sure.

The warriors waited until the black of night, when the Apache campfires glowed like little red stars and the smoke from the a'ut roasting pits curled up gray against the sky. Then they crept into the camp and all at once shouted their terrible war cries.

Imagine the women's frightened scurrying and hopeless attempts to save their children! Actually, they need not have feared for their lives, for it was Pima custom to adopt women and children captives. They were never tortured but treated with all possible kindness.

However, these were days of great poverty for the Indians. Despite his good intentions, sometimes a Pima captor was unable to provide his prisoner with food and other necessities of life. When this happened he had but one logical alternative: sell the captive and use the money to provide for his own family.

Such was the fate of little Wasaja. Just as the five-year-old was adjusting to life in a small village near Sacaton (some say it was Blackwater), and getting to know his new Pima playmates, he was taken to *S-auppagk* (Many Cottonwood Trees), the white man's city of Florence, on horseback in the company of three Pima men.

Here Providence kindly interceded in our little hero's life. It so happened that a young Italian named Charles Gentile was taking a morning stroll down the dusty Florence main street just as the Pimas entered town with their little captive. A man of great culture and some affluence, Mr. Gentile had been educated in the best Italian schools. Later he had taken his share of his inheritance and left to seek his fortune in America, where he became one of the founders of the Chicago Art Institute. He had traveled west on business and was about to return to Chicago in a prairie schooner when he was accosted by the party of Indians.

The Italian's face must have registered shock when he realized what the Pimas were proposing. That Wasaja was not one of their tribe was obvious from the start, for the child still wore his Apache buckskin and moccasins. Later, as the conversation proceeded in Spanish, it became clear that the Pimas were asking the sum of thirty dollars for the boy. Mr. Gentile was a devout Catholic, and such bargaining must have struck him as strangely pagan and barbaric.

Who knows what finally prompted the young art dealer to reach into his pocket for the correct sum to pay for the little Apache. It could have been loneliness, for Charles Gentile was a bachelor. More likely it was compassion, perhaps mixed with a strange prompting from Above. After all, the tale is strangely reminiscent of some of the stories contained in the Old Testament.

In any case, Mr. Gentile's first act was to take Wasaja to his room and give him a good hot bath with a bar of soap. How odd this must have seemed to the little boy who had heretofore bathed only in the cold waters of a river! Next came a change of apparel — a white man's cloth shirt and trousers replaced the buckskin suit and moccasins the child's mother had lovingly made with her own hands.

The third great change was in Wasaja's name. Mr. Gentile took his little charge to the Catholic church, where the priest baptized him and christened him Carlos Montezuma, a name that would someday instill pride in the hearts of his Indian people.

Finally came the change of place. Mr. Gentile helped little Carlos up to perch on the prairie schooner's high seat, and the two set out for far-away Chicago. As the covered wagon left Florence, a touching scene occurred. From the window of a row of adobe houses, the Apache child heard his Indian name called — "Wasaja! Wasaja!" He turned to see his two sisters waving at him. The innocent little boy gave them a happy smile — he had no idea that this was to be the last time he would see his dear ones. (Both sisters also had been captured in the surprise Pima raid at Black Mesa. One was eventually taken to Mexico, where she married a Mexican. The other was taken to California.)

During the long journey Mr. Gentile began to teach little Carlos the English language. The boy soon learned to hold the reins, uttering, "Go, horsey, go!" He always felt a thrill when the horses trotted faster at his command.

After weeks on the road, the two travelers stopped at Grand Rapids, Michigan, while Mr. Gentile made additional art transactions. Then it was on to Chicago, where the young Italian's gallery was located.

In a short time little Carlos had mastered English and made many friends among the street orphans of the Windy

City. With them he played hooky from school to fish on the lake or water the P. T. Barnum elephants. He learned to hitch rides behind buses, and to sell newspapers and shine shoes for pocket money. These early memories caused many a reminiscent chuckle when the Apache boy became a man.

In 1875 Carlos was enrolled in a public school near Galesburg, Illinois. Soon afterward Mr. Gentile moved his gallery to New York, taking his little Indian charge with him and enrolling him in school there. Unfortunately the new gallery burned, and Carlos' benefactor was ruined financially. Although he continued to show a fond interest in his ward, Mr. Gentile was no longer able to support him. At ten years of age little Carlos was left to shift for himself.

He attended elementary school in Brooklyn for one more year. Then he was brought to Urbana, Illinois, where he was tutored in a course preparatory to university enrollment. Two kind retired lady teachers and a Baptist minister named Mr. Stedman helped the young Apache during these hard years, offering him the comfort of their homes in exchange for errand-running and household chores.

Carlos entered the University of Illinois in 1880. To finance his education, he worked at any job he could find and during vacations labored long hours on a farm near Urbana. In 1884 he graduated with a Bachelor of Science degree from the School of Chemistry.

His diploma allowed him to obtain a place in a drugstore in Chicago, where he worked and made his home while he attended lectures in the College of Medicine at Northwestern University. Finally in 1889 Carlos Montezuma received the degrees of Doctor of Medicine and Practical Pharmacist.

General T. J. Morgan, commissioner of Indian Affairs, heard of the young Apache's accomplishment and offered him a position in the Indian Service. The new graduate accepted the offer and was placed at Fort Stevenson, North Dakota, as clerk and physician. He later served at Western Shoshone, Nevada, and Colville Agency, Washington.

Dr. Carlos Montezuma had prepared for his profession well. When the call came from the famous U.S. Indian school in Carlisle, Pennsylvania, he was ready to accept the position of school physician. At Carlisle, Carlos became a warm friend of General R. H. Pratt, the school's founder. The two had the common bond of concern for the Indian race, both believing strongly that the first Americans were not receiving proper treatment. They traveled about the country making rousing speeches — "Stay the Sword; the Indian is a Human Being" by Pratt, and "Let My People Go" by Montezuma.

Often Carlos returned to the desert land of his birth to give his speeches and visit with his cousins, his mother's nephews, Charley and George Dickens of Fort McDowell. These trips must have awakened strong emotions in the doctor.

Once he told me how he used his first savings to return to Sacaton just to meet his Pima captor. He called for a meeting, but the Indian warriors eyed him suspiciously. No one wanted to admit the deed for fear Montezuma would seek revenge.

The doctor tried to convince the braves that he held no rancor. He only wanted to thank his captor for doing him a good deed; without him he would still be an educated person on the reservation.

At last one old warrior timidly left the group and approached Montezuma. The doctor shook his hand, and the old man smiled. (One of my father Red Arrow's old friends witnessed the meeting and once told me how Dr. Montezuma had pressed folded currency into the Pima's wrinkled hand.)

As further visits promoted greater understanding, the Pimas came to wholeheartedly agree that Dr. Carlos Montezuma was a kind and generous Apache with no bitterness in his heart for anyone. Once my husband Ross told me of a group of Salt River old men who called themselves "Montezuma's Friends," so great was their respect for this educated Indian.

One of Dr. Montezuma's greatest desires was to go to Chicago and start an independent practice there. While he was still at Carlisle he wrote a letter of inquiry to one of his non-Indian friends in the Windy City but received a discouraging answer: "If you come to Chicago, I am afraid you will not make a success. Better stay where you are where your job is secure. There will be prejudice against you, even though you may be the best physician — you are an Indian."

Dr. Carlos Montezuma's reaction was defiant. Later he told me, "When I read these words, my Apache blood rushed into my head, and I said, 'God helping me I will resign the Government Service and go back to Chicago and fight prejudice.' I was willing to sacrifice everything for my race. So I took the choice of coming in contact with prejudice and going against the current of life, defying the world for the rights with which God has endowed the Indian race as one of his creatures. I assure you I was not discouraged or dismayed."

Thus, after more than seven years as resident physician at the great Carlisle School, Dr. Carlos Montezuma resigned his position in 1896. He returned to Chicago to crusade for his cause and to set an example for his people. After he found an office in a good location, he proudly hung out a large shingle which read "Dr. Carlos Montezuma, M.D.," in bold letters.

The young doctor worked hard to make good, and soon both rich and poor patients were crowding his office. He demonstrated his kindness and impartiality by treating all races and nationalities alike. Many patients became his friends and fondly called him "Monte." His humanity and humility endeared him to all classes of people.

One day a poor patient told him, "Monte, I am sorry — I cannot pay my bill." The doctor only smiled and told him, "Never mind. Go home and make sure you take your medicine." No sooner was the sick man out of sight than Montezuma requested his receptionist to go to the nearby market and order ten dollars' worth of groceries for the poor patient. "Remember to sign it, 'From the Baptist Church'," he told her. Dr. Montezuma was a devout Baptist, and his humanitarian spirit was often evidenced under the auspices of his church or through the Masonic Order, of which he was also an active member.

The doctor walked alone in his successful profession until he was in his early fifties. Then he met a young German girl, twenty years younger than himself, who had come to America at the age of twelve years with her mother. Dan Cupid's arrow struck so hard that the doctor would not rest until he had asked Miss Marie Keller's hand in marriage. She became a charming wife and a perfect hostess at the frequent gatherings held in their Michigan Avenue apartment, which was always open to their many friends.

Even his active social life did not keep Carlos Montezuma from crusading for his people, however. Freeing the American Indian from the bonds of prejudice was always uppermost in his mind. Once he traveled to Arizona to speak to the Indians of Lehi, with Lancisco Hill as interpreter. "Get rid of the yoke that weighs you from rising to a higher plane!" he invoked his brothers.

The BIA agent at Lehi feared the Indians' reaction to the doctor's disturbing words, and he told an Indian policeman to break up the meeting. The officer threatened to arrest the listeners and throw them in jail; then he seized Dr. Montezuma and escorted him to the outskirts of the reservation. Not in the least bit daunted by this experience, the doctor always recalled it with a chuckle. "Poor Mary sat on top of her suitcase by the road and cried," he said. "She thought I had deserted her to meet the Indians alone!"

Around 1920 Dr. Montezuma was stricken with diabetes, then an incurable disease. He kept his condition from his wife for fear of worrying her, but his steady loss of weight told Mary that something was seriously wrong with her handsome Indian husband. His close friends and Masonic brothers advised him to go to Arizona, where the climate would be good for him. Although hesitant to heed their pleadings, in the end he gave in.

The story of Carlos Montezuma's last days, during some of which I was privileged to nurse him, has already been related in the text of this book. The manner in which this wonderfully determined crusader inspired my husband and me to take up the battle against prejudice ourselves has also already been described, along with an excerpt from one of the doctor's arousing speeches. Yet I wonder if I have been able to truly portray this great man's humility and kindness. And how could I possibly get across the fire and strength of his words?

Dr. Montezuma returned to Arizona in early December; within two months' time he had expired, despite the efforts of the Apache medicine men. During the time he lay dying, many Indians came to see the revered surgeon who had been such an outstanding leader of his people.

John Smith, a Yavapai Apache who was only seven years old at the time and living with Montezuma's relatives, tells a particularly touching story: "When I saw Dr. Montezuma lying on the cold dirt floor of the brush wickiup, I would rekindle the dying embers because I felt sorry for him." Later John became a member of the session of the Presbyterian church at Fort McDowell, a fine family man, and a supervisor in the Phoenix Water Department. He is only one of many Indians who have walked the path of success by following Dr. Montezuma's courageous example.

There was snow on the Four Peaks in the late part of January 1923, when the remains of Wasaja were laid to rest in the cemetery at Fort McDowell. Many years have passed since that day, but the words of this great man still ring out to prod the Indian nation on to progress.

Carlos Montezuma spent most of his life in the white man's world, but his heart was always with his people. He came home to us in his dying days, and it was to us that he uttered his last inspiring words: "Our hearts must throb with love, our souls must reach to God to guide us. In behalf of my people, with the spirit of Moses I ask, 'Let my people go!'"

*   *   *

William Thomas Moore*

I WAS FIVE YEARS OLD in 1924, when my brother Russell and I went to live with Uncle Bill and his wife Mary, the widow of the famous Dr. Carlos Montezuma. Our father had just died, and mother felt it was best to accept our uncle's kind offer to raise and educate us as his own.

Uncle Bill lived in Blue Island, a suburban town sixteen miles south of the Chicago Loop. He had bought his nice new house just before our arrival, and we boys thought it was great fun to live in a fancy home with all the modern facilities of running water, lights, and gas. Uncle Bill's dog Fox soon became my pal, and I liked to pet the big cat who was also a part of the family. Aunt Mary bought me a little red wagon, and I loved to give my cousins Rod and Adeline rides in it when they were visiting us.

My brother and I were quite happy with Uncle Bill and Aunt Mary. Uncle Bill reminded us of our father, who had been so kind and considerate. Like our father, he took us to Sunday school regularly. Aunt Mary was of German heritage, and she cooked delicious German meals. I espe-

---

*This biographical description was contributed by the author's nephew, Everett Moore.

cially loved her chicken and dumplings, sauerkraut, and spareribs.

Uncle Bill used to leave the house each weekday morning to go to work in the big city. He was a cabinet-maker for the telephone company, but his true avocation was music, which he taught in our home. He taught all band instruments, but his specialties were the cornet and violin. Each morning I would awake to hear him softly practicing his cornet, faithfully working at the intricate exercises and solos until they rippled with precision. I wished the whole world could hear him and know of his wonderful ability.

Those who did know him loved and admired him. He was adored by his pupils, for he was a very patient, kind, and considerate teacher. Uncle Bill had the firm belief that no one was actually tone deaf. He felt that everyone could learn to play some musical instrument to a degree. This faith in each student's ability instilled even the most difficult learners with enthusiasm. Soon hard-to-teach students were being referred to Uncle Bill by other musicians.

His clientele came from all walks of life: insurance men, laborers, carpenters, you name it. But one particular pupil aroused my childish fascination for the unusual. Paul was the biggest man I had ever seen — tall and huge with shoulders so broad I used to wonder how he made it through the door. The first time he shook my hand, my little paw disappeared and was crushed in the exuberance of his greeting.

This giant was a jolly person, who always called Uncle Bill by the affectionate names of Willie or Billie. He worshipped the ground my uncle walked on and always declared, "There is no other teacher like Billie."

Readers, it might surprise you to know that this large man was a professional wrestler of renown. I used to marvel that of all possible instruments he chose the fragile violin. It looked like a toy in his huge hands, but Uncle Bill taught him to use it to evoke beautiful melodies as he drew the bow over the strings with his powerful, sausagelike fingers.

I was a puny seven-year-old when Uncle Bill decided to get me started on my musical education. When he placed the cornet in my hands and told me to press it gently to my lips, I was amazed at how heavy it was! Uncle Bill handled the horn as though it were as light as a feather!

I was told how to set my lips, then asked to blow into the mouthpiece. My first attempt was hopelessly weak. Uncle Bill told me to blow harder and to hold on to the tone. I tried, and my tone was better, but I was beginning to feel weak from blowing so hard. My face must have turned red or purple; the horn gradually dropped until it pointed to the floor. Finally I fell over in a dead faint.

So Uncle Bill tried me on the violin. "This should be easy," I thought. "I don't have to blow."

My uncle showed me how to tuck the violin under my chin, holding the instrument with my left hand and moving the bow with my right. I tried hard to learn the new actions, but my movements were stiff, my nerves felt taut, and I ached all over.

After I had learned to draw the bow over the strings I was shown how to finger the scale. This was just too much! A feeling of shame and inadequacy came over me. I was simply too dumb to learn music! Despair welled in my eyes. Just then I was saved as Aunt Mary called, "Soup's on! Come and eat!"

I was more than willing to give up the idea of learning music, for I thought I was a hopeless case. My clumsy attempts only embarrassed me before the man I so admired. But Uncle Bill was not one to give up so easily.

Sunday dinners were always special at our house, for Aunt Mary would prepare German-style chicken and dumplings and one or more of Uncle Bill's musical friends would join us for dinner. After we ate, the musicians would move to the living room to play their instruments until supper time.

One Sunday shortly after my violin disaster, Uncle Bill introduced us to a foreign-looking gentleman named Mr. Kannette. He was a well-known concert pianist from the Balkan countries, and his stiffly formal dress and impeccable manners impressed me.

After our usual cake and gelatin desert, Uncle Bill and Mr. Kannette excused themselves and went into the living room to play. Our guest warmed up at the keyboard with a light minuet, while Uncle Bill began the ceremony of tuning his violin. When they finally felt that all was ready, the two launched into an amazing spontaneous musical program which held me enthralled. First came a medley of waltzes; then we heard selections from Brahms, Beethoven, Haydn, Chopin, and Liszt.

Off and on throughout the afternoon I caught my Uncle Bill beaming at me with satisfaction. Perhaps he had planned the entire program to test my reactions. In any case, it was easy to see my admiration as I watched the pianist's nimble fingers dancing lightly over the keys.

Imagine my excitement when Uncle Bill announced at supper that I would take piano lessons from Mr. Kannette! Learning to play was a slow and demanding process, but

I practiced for long hours with pleasure. I learned to love the great composers and gradually gained enough confidence to take up other instruments. In high school I played first-chair clarinet and was president of the school band. But my favorite was always the piano, which I played in the dance orchestra. Eventually I became good enough on the keyboard to have the honor of accompanying Uncle Bill during his violin solos.

Uncle Bill as a soloist was a perfectionist. He practiced each selection over and over again until he had it exactly right. But he was never smug or boastful about his accomplishments. I will always remember the quiet, modest manner he would assume as he waited for me to play the introduction to one of his solos. This quiet attitude was so typical that if you were hearing him for the first time you would be taken unaware at what followed. His fine musicianship and skillful execution would make you sit up and take notice. His tone was so pure, his fingering so easy and effortless, his phrasing so beautiful! I was proud and yet humble to be privileged to play with such a great musician.

As I write this description of the wonderful man who raised me I realize that I am not only writing of a man but of a way of life. Once as we were waiting for an elevated train after one of my uncle's solo engagements, he summed up his philosophy for me. I was in a reverie, recalling the wonderful music, the warm applause, my uncle's modest manner. Suddenly I realized that Uncle Bill had spoken to me. I turned to him, and he repeated what he had said: "Everett, always remember this. If you can do anything well, you don't have to tell anyone. When the time comes to do it, then do it."

Later I came to understand and appreciate how my uncle applied this principle in his own life. Anything he did he tried to do well, and he worked hard at becoming a better person all the time. A story once related to me by Uncle Bill's schoolmates illustrates this characteristic.

The school band was rehearsing a concert selection which featured a beautiful baritone solo. The soloist had not showed up, and the director asked if someone would be willing to fill in.

No one said a word. Then Bill Moore raised his hand from the trombone section. The director looked at him inquisitively and shrugged his shoulders as if to say, "Well, he will be better than nothing."

So Uncle Bill began to warm up on the baritone. When the cue for the solo came, he raised the horn to his lips and played the melody without a flaw. His tone had a beautiful round timbre to it, and his performance astonished the whole band.

When my uncle had finished, the director stopped the music. He bowed his head for a moment, took off his glasses, wiped his eyes, and blew his nose. Then he gave Uncle Bill the finest compliment anyone could offer: "That was the best rendition of that solo I have ever heard." You see, Uncle Bill had been practicing the baritone alone, without anyone knowing it.

My uncle's quiet striving for perfection was evident in all phases of his life. He was particularly proud of his health, and often we would don old sweatshirts, shorts, and sneakers for a run around the cinder path in the nearby park. He ate sparingly to lose weight, although to me he looked pretty trim. He abhorred smoking and drinking. For a long time he kept a bottle of whiskey for medicinal purposes, but one day he told Aunt Mary to throw it in the garbage can. He never took medicines and refused all pain-killers during a tooth extraction.

Because he took so long to make a decision, he was determined to stick by it. Once he had made up his mind, no one could influence or dominate him. Once after he received his army bonus he announced he was going to buy a car and learn to drive it. We waited and waited for him to make a choice. Many of his friends tried to sell him their own cars at terrific bargains, but he turned them all down.

Finally Aunt Mary bought an old Chevy without consulting him. She asked the dealer to park it in back of the house so she could surprise her husband. When Uncle Bill returned from work that evening, she proudly showed him her purchase.

Uncle Bill took one look and without a word walked into the house. He shut himself in the bedroom and refused to come to supper. Aunt Mary and I ate a quiet and somewhat embarrassed meal. Later that night I overheard my aunt asking, "Bill, why don't you like the car? It was such a bargain!"

Uncle Bill kept his peace and never uttered a word. The little green car stood beside the house for a month looking very forlorn and unwanted. My aunt finally had it towed away.

One day as Aunt Mary was working in the flower garden and I was cutting the grass, a shiny new Buick drove up to the house and stopped with a loud blare of the horn. There sat Uncle Bill in the driver's seat, smiling and telling us to get in for a spin. Aunt Mary was all eyes. Uncle Bill drove off as if he had been driving all his life. In this instance as well as in his music, he had practiced to attain perfection with no one knowing. It had taken him a long time to make his decision, but once he had made it he knew what he wanted and set out to get his dream. He simply would not settle for second best.

Uncle Bill's determination to aim for the highest goal served him well all his life. He was proud to be a full-blood Indian, but he chose to live in an atmosphere completely foreign to his native reservation. He lived the life of a white man to the best of his ability in order to set an example for his Indian people.

His dedication to helping others cannot be adequately described here. I believe that this great musician could have been famous, but his main desire was to inspire others. Surely he more than succeeded in this goal, as he passed his wonderful talent and wisdom on to all who knew him, by music, by word, and by deed.

*   *   *

Russell "Big Chief" Moore

IN 1912, IN AN OLAS KIH on a remote part of the Gila River Reservation, a healthy baby boy was born. Who would have thought he was to become a world-famous jazz musician and ambassador for his Indian people?

Even as a toddler Russell Moore's love of music was apparent. His earliest memory is of his grandfather singing the old Pima chants. He fashioned a homemade flute

from an old piece of pipe and went about the village toot-
ing band tunes on it. Finally his parents hid the instrument
in order to get some peace and quiet.

Another major facet of Russell's personality — his sense
of humor and love of jokes — was also evident during his
early childhood. Once he tried to fool his grandparents
when he visited them. *"Nam ia thadha al kekel?* (Are you
old people here?)" he asked outside their door in a disguised voice. His grandmother got up to let the stranger
in, but his grandfather saw through the joke and told her,
"Don't let Russell fool you!" Sure enough, in came their
grandson laughing.

When he was ten years old he wanted to learn to be a
barber. He tried to cut his playmates' hair, but they soon
shied away from his scissors. Only his grandfather
remained to be practiced on.

One evening the old one was resting on a mat under
the brush ramada. Russell approached him with his shears
and asked to cut his hair. "My *wosmad* (grandson), I'm
too tired to sit up," objected the old gentleman.

"Aw! that's *s-ap'e* (all right)," replied the good-natured
boy. "I'll just trim while you're lying down." So the bud-
ding young barber squatted low and cut one side and
then the other.

Soon after this event Russ' father passed away, and he
and his little brother Everett were sent to live with their
Uncle Bill in Blue Island, a suburb of Chicago. Bill saw
to it that Russ learned to play the piano as well as several
brass instruments.

From the beginning of his musical education the boy
showed a preference for jazz. Frequently he was caught

practicing jazz pieces instead of the classical numbers his piano teacher had assigned. He was always reprimanded for this, but the lectures only served to make him more determined. He spent many of his nights in the big city, going from nightclub to nightclub, listening to the jazz greats.

After he returned to Arizona to enroll in the Phoenix Indian School, Russ' interest in jazz continued to develop. The band leader there allowed the boy to practice modern music to his heart's content. By 1935, when Russell graduated from the Sherman Institute in Riverside, California, he was determined to make a career as a jazz trombonist.

His first step into the big time came when he joined Lionel Hampton's band right after graduation. After five years with this group, he set out for New York. Oscar "Papa" Celestin helped him polish his style, and Sidney Bechet taught him to play traditional Dixieland. But the major influence on his career was his close friend Louis Armstrong. The skillful and moving trombone solos he played as part of "Satchmo's" band brought him worldwide fame.

Russ traveled to Europe to take part in jazz festivals, and he toured the world with Armstrong. Later he formed his own bands in Philadelphia and Columbus. It was a thrill for us folks back home to see this great Pima perform on the television shows of such well-known personalities as Ed Sullivan and Mike Douglas.

As he grew older, Russ gave up the hectic life of touring to settle down in a small New York town with his Oneida Indian wife Ida and his two fine children, Randy and Amy. However, he never stopped making recordings, writing new jazz numbers, and performing feature spots at various nightclubs.

Throughout his career Russell remembered his Indian heritage. Every few years he would return to the reservation to play jazz for his people, eat the old Indian foods, and learn more of the traditional Pima chants, which he put on phonograph records. We always looked forward to hearing his wonderful music and laughing at his lively sense of humor.

His love of a joke was something Russ never lost. He had us all in stitches when he spoke at our first national Indian trade fair in 1967. The funny memories he conjured up were common to us all — going barefoot on the hot desert sand, his first shoes at the Phoenix Indian School, his squabbles with the school disciplinarian, getting up at 5:00 A.M. to milk the cows. What Indian doesn't remember such incidents? But it takes a Russell Moore to relate them in a truly side-splitting way.

Russell's love of his Indian people can be seen in his concern for them. In the early 1970s he toured Indian schools all over the country, coaxing Indian children to study music. He believes that almost all Indians have musical ability, and he hopes to see more of them cultivate this talent professionally.

Russ' own highly successful career can certainly serve as inspiration for musically inclined young Indians. And on a broader level, his ability to transcend racial barriers can instill courage in all our people. Russell has numbered among his closest friends people of all races and has functioned as an equal among world-famous personalities. He has proved that the Indian is not inferior, but a person of talent, dignity, and stature. We are all grateful to have such an outstanding example to follow.

*   *   *

Dr. Roe Blaine Lewis

IN THE 1880s IN A little adobe church on the sun-baked desert near Sacaton, the determined Dr. C. H. Cook reaped his first converts. Among them was a man whom the pastor christened John Lewis. How it would gladden Dr. Cook's heart if he could see the Christian family pattern this baptism engendered!

John Lewis was a dedicated Christian, and he saw to it that his children received good Christian training. One of his sons, Richard, attended the Tucson Mission School, the C. H. Cook Christian Training School, and the Moody Bible Institute. He became a missionary in Papago land, where he met and married a talented pianist named Susan Blaine.

The minister lived to see the birth of two fine sons but passed away when the boys were very young. Dick, the youngest, paid the supreme sacrifice in World War II and was buried in the Marshall Islands. Roe was left to comfort his mother and follow in his father's Christian footsteps.

After he graduated with a B.S. in education from Arizona State University, Roe Lewis organized and developed a modern school of agriculture at the Phoenix Indian School. Later he went to the Maricopa Colony on the Gila River Reservation as principal of the BIA institution there. He married Sallie Sims and became the father of three sons, Robert, Rodney, and John.

But Roe was not content in his educational profession. At night the desert breeze seemed to call to him: *"G wo i hihim!* (come!)" It was clear that his soul would not rest until he too had taken up his father's Christian calling.

Thus it was that the young man resigned his position at the BIA school, packed up his family, and set out for the San Francisco Theological Seminary in San Anselmo, California. There he served as pastor in a nearby church while he completed his theological training with special emphasis on sociology and economics.

At last Roe returned to Arizona and was ordained at Vah-aki, where he served until he was called to teach rural church courses at the C. H. Cook Christian Training School in Phoenix. This opportunity gave him the chance to combine his abilities as a minister and an educator, and he organized the department of the rural church at the Cook School.

In 1954 Reverend Lewis became pastor of the Phoenix Indian Presbyterian Church. Two years later he again combined his two professions as an educational counselor for Indian youth on the staff of the Board of the National Indian Missions of the United Presbyterian Church. This position later led him to serve as educational field counselor for the board, traveling about the country as a friend, teacher, and counselor to Indians of all tribes.

The honorary degree of Doctor of Divinity was bestowed upon Dr. Roe B. Lewis by the University of Dubuque, Iowa, in 1966, making him the first Pima-Papago Indian to reach the highest rank in theology. How fitting it was that at last this great man was a *mahkai,* a doctor, a title he had well earned with his patience and love for his fellowmen.

*　　*　　*

Mae Fern Perkins

MAY 7, 1969, WILL NEVER be forgotten by a lovely Pima maiden named Mae Fern Perkins. On that day her parents, Mr. and Mrs. George Perkins of Blackwater, proudly watched their daughter receive her stewardess' wings from TWA.

Although the way was hard and filled with all the homesickness of her first time away from home, Mae Fern had passed her difficult exam with the remarkable grade of 97.07. She served her airline well, a fine inspiration for her Pima sisters, until she became Mrs. K. Witkowski and settled down to raise a family in Illinois.

Mae Fern's paternal grandfather, the late Crouse Perkins, was a graduate of the C. H. Cook Christian Training School. Her maternal great-grandfather, James Ellis, was also a C. H. Cook School product. It is interesting to note this family's pattern of achievement.

*   *   *

Brigadier General George Stewart Cassady

SOMETIMES IT HAPPENS that a non-Indian becomes filled with such compassion and dedication to the Indian cause that our people cease to see him as different from themselves. For all practical purposes he has become one of us, and we place our deepest trust in him.

Such a man was retired U.S. Air Force Brigadier General George Stewart Cassady, who served as tribal general business manager for our Salt River Indian Community from 1962–65. During his time of service he displayed unparalleled enthusiasm, dedication, and devotion. The results of his work can be seen everywhere — in a fine gasoline service station, our Tri-Community Landfill Operation, our Mutual Self-Help homes, and in many other projects.

Once in 1965 General Cassady accidently discovered that our beautiful McDowell Mountain Range, for so long loved by Pimas and Apaches alike, had been sold by the government to a private company. We had never even been consulted. What an outrage!

When he returned to Phoenix, General Cassady wrote a boldly protesting article to appear in the Phoenix newspaper. Like us, he was heartbroken and disgusted by the transaction, and he wanted the world to know it.

General Cassady thought so much like us that he came to call us "his people." When he was taken from us in a tragic auto accident on November 9, 1966, we were filled with sadness and deep sorrow at our loss. As was his desire, he was interred in our Salt River tribal burial grounds, among the people he had helped so much.

My beloved late grandnephew Raymond W. Wilson was moved to write the following poem, which aptly summarizes our feelings upon General Cassady's death:

Sufficiency of God's Grace

In Memory of our Friend, General Cassady

God's grace is sufficient,
    What is there to fear?
Life's storms may prevail,
    Tribal problems may seem difficult,

But God controls and eases each one,
    That confronts me daily,
And silently and softly he whispers,
    "The Great Shepherd Doth Know."

God's grace is sufficient,
    So why should I quail,
Though the dark clouds are slowly rising,
Though the shadows are drawing nigh,
God's grace is sufficient and boundless
    To protect and carry me through,
I'll be safe in his bosom,
    As he softly calls me into the fold.

God's love is sufficient,
    It is endless and free,
As high as the Four Peaks in the east,
    Countless as the sand in the dry Salt River bottom,
Here among my beloved Pima Indians I will rest
    Till the darkness is no more
And awake in his likeness,
    To abide forever in eternal bliss.